BUILDING THE PERFECT ANIMAL

NEW & SELECTED POEMS (1993–2023)

Also by C. Dale Young

Prometeo
The Affliction (novel)
The Halo
Torn
The Second Person
The Day Underneath the Day

BUILDING THE PERFECT ANIMAL

NEW & SELECTED POEMS (1993–2023)

C. DALE YOUNG

FOUR WAY BOOKS
TRIBECA

In memory of my father

Library of Congress Cataloging-in-Publication Data

Names: Young, C. Dale, author.
Title: Building the perfect animal : new and selected poems / C. Dale Young.
Description: New York : Four Way Books, 2025.
Identifiers: LCCN 2024035182 (print) | LCCN 2024035183 (ebook) | ISBN
9781961897328 (trade paperback) | ISBN 9781961897335 (ebook)
Subjects: LCGFT: Poetry.
Classification: LCC PS3625.O96 B85 2025 (print) | LCC PS3625.O96 (ebook)
| DDC 811/.6—dc23/eng/20240813
LC record available at https://lccn.loc.gov/2024035182
LC ebook record available at https://lccn.loc.gov/2024035183
This book is manufactured in the United States of America and printed on
acid-free paper.

Four Way Books is a not-for-profit literary press. We are grateful for the assistance
we receive from individual donors, public arts agencies, and private foundations
including the New York State Council on the Arts, a state agency.

We are a proud member of the Community of Literary Magazines and Presses.

Selections from *The Day Underneath the Day* copyright 2001 by C. Dale Young.
Published 2001 by TriQuarterly Books/Northwestern University Press.

Contents

BUILDING THE PERFECT ANIMAL

SELECTED POEMS

Building the Perfect Animal

Four arms, four legs, and a head with two faces, Zeus feared humans were the perfect animal and split them into two separate parts, condemning them to spend their lives in search of their other halves.

—Plato, *The Symposium*

Memento

The heart flickered within the chest
and generated heat, a tiny version of the sun
placed in the center of the chest by God.

And therein we find the first fabrication.
The second? That the heart was the seat
of a man's soul. So strong was this belief

that Galen insisted the heart was
most important among organs, detailed how
tiny pores in the septum of the heart

allowed blood to seep from one side to the other.
So adamant was Galen that centuries later
clear-eyed Da Vinci and even Vesalius

chose to depict these pores despite the fact
neither one observed them. Sometimes
belief overrides truth. In their filthy journals,

the early missionaries recorded the way
Aztec priests ripped the hearts of men and women
out after cutting through their ribs in a single slice.

But this cannot be true. The ribs are a better armor
than many realize. The priests made a quick slice
from the umbilicus up and through the diaphragm

to reveal the beating heart at the bottom of the chest,
visualizing it clearly before extracting it.
Once the heart was removed, they kept it

while discarding the body, the feeble thing
tumbling down the steps of the pyramid.
When a patient tells me her heart hurts, I know

she is not having physical pain. I have studied
figuration almost as much as I have studied the heart.
The heart longs, flutters like a bird, and even sings.

She says her heart hurts so much it brings tears
to her eyes. And I nod to acknowledge her truth.
What else can I do? I have not held my beloved

in my arms as he gasped and died. You see,
her husband had heart failure, fluid filling his chest
more quickly than the medicines could help remove it.

He drowned. On land and breathing air, his heart
failed him and he drowned. And when my patient
tells me she kept her husband's heart, kept the

bloated heart that failed him in a box lined with
red velvet befitting a king, red velvet trimmed with
white rabbit fur, more than a small part of me believes her.

Myth

Of course it begins with loneliness…
What did you expect? When my father
tells the story, he starts at the beginning because
this, as he says, is what one does. The goddess

Atabey lived alone for almost an eternity.
She created humans and all manner of animals,
but the loneliness remained. The loneliness
sat with her the way close family does.

Eventually, her loneliness grew so large she
laid herself down and formed twins within her,
twin gods she delivered unto the world. One
became the sea god, the other the god of the harvest.

These gods brought comfort to Atabey,
so much so she brought other gods into the world.
My father says Guacar, the god of the harvest,
became overworked from humans planting more

and more crops. He realized the only way to keep up
was to sacrifice himself. He descended El Yunque
and went out into the fields. There he drew
the machete across his neck and bled into the earth.

Yúcahu, the sea god, searched the entire world
for his twin. He could feel his presence everywhere
but could not find him. Yúcahu mourned.
And soon he, too, understood loneliness.

When a boy is born prematurely, one takes him
to the sea to ask the sea god's protection.
And so, millennia ago, a boy was born early
and his parents took him to the sea. The sea god

granted the child protection. But soon, another
family brought their premature son, and when Yúcahu
wrapped him in protection it created a thread
to the previous boy, the two boys inadvertently linked.

The two found each other and were inseparable.
People called them "the brothers." For the rest
of their lives, they could not remain apart for long.
Even after they were grown men with their own families,

these two had to see each other, had to be
with each other, so powerful was this thread.
And then the day came when, in old age, one
of these brothers passed away. The remaining

brother grieved. He could not imagine life
without his brother. He went to the sea and prayed
to Yúcahu, prayed for him to bring his brother back.
The sea god, who understood such grief, agreed

but under one condition: the man had to sacrifice
himself, had to offer the thing of highest worth
he still possessed. But what good was life without
his brother? And so, the man walked into the sea

and drowned. Soon, another couple brought their
premature son, and the sea god placed a part of himself
and one of the brothers in him. And eventually,
another couple brought their son, and Yúcahu placed

part of himself and the other brother within him.
Over and over, the brothers, the twins, are reborn.
Over and over, they find each other and cannot remain apart.
My father says there is no moral to this story, none.

I say the story is about love, powerful love that
transcends even death. Think about it. Why do they
always find each other and then cannot be apart?
Why is it as long as they are together the sea god

feels less lonely? Inside each of these boys
Yúcahu placed a part of himself, a desperate attempt
to recreate the twin god he lost. So I tell you: I was born
prematurely. I was taken to the sea to ensure I was protected.

I am drawn to the sea, and I have never lived
far from it. It comforts me the way family does for some.
And today, as I stand on this beach staring at the sea,
I can feel the god within me reverberating.

Self-Portrait Using Three Mirrors, 2021

after David Hockney

But, tell me, when have I not loved difficulty?
Unlike Parmigianino who stared directly at himself,
a convex mirror is simply not enough for me.

I want not distortion but an exaggerated sense
of detail: I want me and not my facile idea of me.
In order to see myself honestly, in order to capture

myself with a natural and somewhat relaxed face,
I had no choice but to use three. Each mirror
is its own difficulty, each bringing another detail

to the forefront. At twenty-two I painted flowers,
but even then I chose to go out and study the branch
of hibiscus outside my window. I needed to see it

from different angles. You would be amazed
what can be seen when you choose to view something
outside of its given frame. My shirt removed,

my pants as well, I sit in my underwear and socks
because I am slightly modest modeling for myself.
Now, I see the grey hairs on my chest, the blemish

on my shoulder. I see the paunch of my belly,
the love handles, the unseemly bulge that
has embarrassed me since adolescence. Naïve then,

I painted with the help of a single mirror, my brush
left to exaggerate the hard angles of my abdomen.
Now, a trio of mirrors shows me just how ordinary

I am. Some say my face is anything but ordinary,
so I paint myself in profile. Three mirrors grant me
my wish, and for once I do not see myself as wretched.

Henceforth

after Jaime Gil de Biedma

All of my life, I could barely remember it. As after a dream,
I stared at the clouds floating above the sea and thought
of rain, and it rained. Later, when I learned the word *Desistare*

and used it with intent, I found I could stop the rain.
"All of my life." It sounds so odd to say that out loud.
But strange thing after strange thing transpired. Imagine.

The day ends in a flash of color and wonder, and the sea
slowly becomes the night sky. You may or may not
have feelings when this happens. I cannot speak for you.

You are still waiting for the antecedent of the first "it."
I can tell you "it" is not the sea tugging at me the way
the moon inflicts its needs upon the tides. The gods

were lonely. And one of them missed his dead brother
so terribly, he placed part of himself inside a human being.
Even I found this unbelievable until one day I met

someone just as capable of conjuring things the way
I can, who carries inside him the same needy god.
I have already said too much. The sea is crashing now

against the coastline demanding silence. For thousands
of years, I have listened to the sea. I never tire of it.
The sea percusses and sounds. The sea detonates.

The Shadow Cast

Golden Gate Park

As any poet will tell you, the weight of the line
is essential, but here these practitioners have
more on their minds than poems. The weight

of their lines is uniformly light, the line selected
to land and then rest gently on the surface,
its goal to capture the attention of surface-feeders

found in nearby lakes. Back and forth, back and forth,
the arm swings repetitively, predictably, the line
then cast out and over the pond until it comes to rest.

In the late morning sunlight, the great trees
littering the pools with shadow, these students
of sorcery practice unspooling their lines, their craft.

We have come not to study magic but to escape
the boredoms of another Saturday morning.
Slowly, we take a lap around the pools.

Back and forth, the casters execute the motion—
they do it as a way to memorize the feel of it,
their movements simple and clear. But just as we have

grown accustomed to this sight, the arm swinging
the line out in a swift but strident way, we spy
a man suddenly whipping his arm side to side and then

in circles, wider and wider the circles, the motion
violently quick and as fluid as a gymnast pulling ribbons.
When he completes the chaos and snaps his arm, the line

catapults. It turns out distance and gravity can be
overcome, the circular motion of the shadow caster
rapidly building energy and torque so that when he

snaps the final motion the line accelerates out, out,
and much farther than the simpler motion allows.
We circle and gawk. We cannot help but show surprise.

What we have witnessed is a proof of physics, but it feels
as if we have been privy to something unbelievable:
a manipulation, a moment, a tiny bit of powerful magic.

Melancholia

The whirring internal machine, its gears
grinding not to a halt but to a pace that emits
a low hum, steady, almost imperceptible:
the Greeks would not have seen it this way.

Simply put, it was a result of black bile,
the small fruit of the gallbladder perched
under the liver somehow over-ripened
and then becoming fetid. So the ancients

would have us believe. But the overly-emotional
and contrarian Romans saw it as a kind of mourning
for one's self. I trust the ancients but I have never
given any of this credence because I cannot understand

how one does this, mourn one's self.
Down by the shoreline—the Pacific
wrestling with far more important
philosophical issues—I recall the English notion

of it being a wistfulness, something John Donne
wore successfully as a fashion statement.
But how does one wear wistfulness well
unless one is a true believer?

The humors within me are unbalanced,
and I doubt they were ever really in balance
to begin with, ever in that rare but beautiful
thing the scientists call equilibrium.

My gallbladder squeezes and wrenches,
or so I imagine. I am wistful and morose
and I am certain black bile is streaming
through my body as I walk beside this seashore.

The small birds scrambling away from the advancing
surf; the sun climbing overhead shortening shadows;
the sound of the waves hushing the cries of gulls:
I have no idea where any of this ends up.

To be balanced, to be without either
peaks or troughs: do tell me what that is like…
This contemplating, this mulling over, often leads
to a moment a few weeks from now,

the one in which everything suddenly shines
with clarity, where my fingers race to put down
the words, my fingers so quick on the keyboard
it will seem like a goddamned miracle.

The Grief of Achilles

Very few dispute that his mother dipped him
in the River Styx to ensure immortality, the spot
on his heel she held left vulnerable and soft.

Nor do many dispute Achilles as an outstanding
warrior, capable of killing even the great Hector.
No, the disputes arise when the name Patroclus

is mentioned in relation to Achilles. We know
from Aeschylus and Plato that they shared
the same tent, and that each had a love for the other

unrivaled by common lovers. But for many,
the very idea two skilled warriors could have
loved each other is unthinkable: friends, close friends,

like brothers, they say. I don't mean to be crass,
but Achilles and Patroclus fucked. There is no
getting around this. Warriors or not, they fucked.

When Patroclus died in battle, slain by the great Hector,
Achilles' grief was severe and larger than any man
could bear, even a man who was a demigod.

He was warned. He was told that to avenge his great love meant risk of death, but his grief was deep and powerful, and he put on his armor and eventually killed Hector.

Round and around Troy he dragged Hector's dead body. And the prophecy came to pass, a single arrow piercing his heel, the one spot on which his mortality rested.

Love takes many forms. And when the beloved is taken, the grief is one few can survive. Achilles did not survive it. He bawled, he put on his armor; he died for Patroclus.

Building the Perfect Animal

An animal will do what it finds necessary
to protect itself. As a child, in books and on television,
I saw the drama of it. You were hurt and needed
protection, but I could not provide it.

The duck-billed platypus was likely designed to be
the perfect animal, but nature had different ideas,
and, well... I won't compare myself to nature
because I am not capable of such fierceness or longevity.

And this is what I should have said, but I didn't.
I dwelled in the hurt, instead, because it felt right.
The Pacific gossiped in the distance, and I cared
then too much about what others thought.

On a day like any other, you simply vanished.
I want to compare it to the way a meerkat avoids danger,
but there is only so far I can push the simile. Let us say
I simply could not see the dangers you were avoiding.

They say the orca evolved from wolves, that they hunt
in the same way wolves do, in packs, with a coordinated
strategy. We cannot help but find this amazing, wolves
repeatedly entering the sea until they were transformed.

Who doesn't want to believe in transformation?
Who doesn't want to believe that with time one evolves
into a better person? Such beliefs help us to survive.
I say these beliefs are cold and ignore the animal.

We are animals, after all, and should remember that.
Failure upon failure, we excelled at failing each other.
We were young and hungry. We didn't understand
how much it took to build the perfect animal.

As If from the Sea

Because this is a dream, the beach is completely
empty, and not a single person can be seen
swimming in the bay. And so I swim as God intended,
au natural, naked or, as we said when we were kids,
nekkid. This nekkidness is the one aspect that happens
in dream as well as in waking life, but that is, well,
irrelevant. This isn't a poem about me swimming
nekkid. I mean, let's be real, I have some standards.
But the sea is calm, almost like a lake, and the water
so clear it is easy to make out small fish darting
in little clusters nearby. The whole thing is so
goddamned peaceful and blissy. But then a man
almost as brown as I am, with a fairly neat mustache,
rises as if he is the man from Atlantis, rises as if
he had been swimming underwater for like a month,
rises and exhales with all the drama of a drag queen.
Okay, that may be pushing it a bit too far, but he
stands and breathes heavily for almost ten minutes before
swimming over to me. He says: "You know why I am here."
But I honestly have no idea. This may be my dream,
but I am never in control in my dreams. When I say never,
I really mean never. Soon, we are kissing, our naked bodies
touching. We are completely inappropriate, but this
isn't about impropriety, nor is it about sex. But we have sex.

And while I am inside him, while we are kissing
and his arms are around my neck, it begins. Our hands
begin twisting together and, without warning, our chests
merge. We twist and fuse and then the dark bark
begins rising from our skin, now one, one body, and
one skin now covered in bark. And this is awesome
in the old-school sense of the word, you know, as
in awe-inspiring, filled with awe. And lo and behold,
we are a single tree standing in the shallows, our feet
now rooted in the sand as the leaves begin erupting
from our branches. That two men having sex
become a tree standing in the sea might seem odd,
but I read a lot of Ovid as child. And well, it
affected me quite deeply. I'm just trying to be
honest here. I mean, I feel I owe you that.
But when I wake, I am covered in sweat, my heart
racing and panicked. I lie there feeling the motion
of the sea within me, my skin prickling, my skin
softened and salty as if from the sea.

Self-Portrait Using a Single Mirror

To study oneself is to see the inverse, the left
now right, your smile crooked in the other direction.
I see what others see and not what I desire.

So, an hour after sunrise, when the morning light is
most flattering, I sit and study my face in this mirror,
study how time has changed it. Time changes

everyone, but most do not see it until they are surprised
by an image caught by someone else on camera.
I need truth. I need to know the impression I offer up

if I intend to paint myself. There was a time I would have
painted myself in a heroic and exaggerated fashion,
but now I choose a realistic pose, one that feels warm

even if I am not. I model for myself. I figure I may as well
model for somebody. Rembrandt loved to model for himself,
loved to give himself his own stern and direct gaze.

For him, it was a means of documentation, a way of proving
he had been here. I do not need such documentation.
I just need to feel seen, even if only by a casual observer

like myself. Outside, the sun is rising quickly, and the
whitecaps on the ocean are now visible and bright.
The greens of things step forward and show their differences.

My face is too bland in this light and at this angle.
What I need is contrast, the sun high above so that shadows
shade the contour of my nose, accentuate my cheekbones.

Some might see this as narcissism, but it is merely a study
in chiaroscuro. Come midafternoon, come the high light,
I will return to my face fully prepared to capture its darkness.

Adrenaline

God of panic, god of safety, you
who gifted us this chemical to ensure,
in a moment's notice, we can fight or flee,
I come now to plead mercy.

The small fruits you left above our kidneys
now refuse to stop firing off their messages.
Night after night, I cannot calm myself,
these glands meant to protect me now

keeping me on high alert. When I fall into dream,
I am again at the hospital walking the long
path toward the double doors.
And as in waking life, the question rises:

Will this be the day, the day I get infected?
Even in sleep, I am managing my patients' panic.
I come now to ask for even one night's relief.
Let me slumber long enough to find myself

at the end of the dock, the blue Caribbean
the only thing in front of me. Let me sit pretending
to fish when all I am doing is studying
the myriad shades of blue I took for granted

for so long. Let the man I love come check on me,
come kiss me on the back of my neck.
Just for one night, let there be no virus,
nothing to worry about except rain clouds advancing.

The Salvation of Patroclus

Because he was angered during a game and killed
a boy, because his competitive side could not be
reined in, the son of Menoetius was deemed

unsalvageable and then discarded, given at a young age
to Peleus, father of Achilles. The boy was incapable
of being raised by a man untrained in war. Menoetius

knew the boy could not be saved. Patroclus was only
two years older than Achilles, and people saw them
as brothers, as twins. They studied together, trained

together, laughed together, bathed each other,
and when their bodies began to change, each put his
mouth to the other. It was inevitable. Each boy saw

the other as a god, as something worthy of praise.
Each of them wanted to be part of the other and,
with time, each accepted the other's seed inside him.

They found themselves bound to each other. When the war
turned against the Greeks, the Trojans threatening
to destroy everything, Patroclus convinced Achilles

to let him lead the army into battle. Only Patroclus could
have done this. In what was an unthinkable act, Achilles
took off his famed armor and placed it on his beloved,

the armor feared by all and a symbol of the man himself.
We know what happened next. Patroclus is killed despite
the divine armor of Achilles. The armor did not save him.

It never could. You see, Patroclus was already saved,
not by armor but by a boy named Achilles who loved him,
gave him the most precious thing he possessed, himself.

The Falling Man

The story is missing, so I fill it in—
it's what a thinking person does to cope.
Without the details, only Death can win.

And so, the panic invariably set in,
the fires on lower floors extinguishing hope.
The story is missing, so I fill it in.

Standing on a desk, he chose the lesser sin.
The floor, too hot to stand on, began to slope.
Without the details, only Death can win.

The shattered glass, the beams then caving in,
could anyone sane maintain a shred of hope?
The story is missing, so I fill it in.

I need to know the way his mind gave in
as smoke engulfed the room. Who could cope?
Without the details, only Death can win.

And out the window, like the smoke's fin,
he flew. He plunged to something green like hope.
Without the details, only Death can win.
The story is missing, so I fill it in.

The Giant

Like the heart, they were not removed from
the recently deceased, the ancient Egyptians
choosing, instead, to mummify them. One needed
a heart and two kidneys to travel to the other world.

When Vesalius examined them, he saw them
as two scales on either side of the heart as fulcrum,
biased as he was by the Bible to view them
as part of a system of conscience or judgment.

Nature's redundancy, you can live with only one.
But as with all things human, there is always
a risk of failure. Failure, after all, being human.
When my father's legs began to swell,

we all thought it was just age, swelling due
to a lack of movement. The adult human kidney
has roughly a million nephrons, each working
to filter our blood and control fluid volumes.

Tirelessly, these organs work 24 hours per day.
We expect them to keep doing this because hope
is also an innate human trait. My father did not
stop swelling. Both of his kidneys were failing,

had done all they could do in a single life.
The fluid slowly built up in his tissues.
And soon his lungs began to fill. To see him
gasping, to see him struggling to breathe,

this man who had lived a life filled with strong
judgments, it seemed impossible. The seat of judgment,
the seat of conscience, the organs that made him
judge me so forcefully, so severely. The irony of it all.

The Romans called them *renes*, which in English became
"reins," the things that reined us in, reined in others.
My nature meant I was weak, a weak man who could not
be reined in. But that was many years ago, almost

a lifetime. So many things said, and then
so many silences. And the last thing he said to me?
"I know who you are now. Forgive me, I was wrong.
You might be the strongest of all my children."

But all things come to an end, even one's father. I kissed
his forehead. I held his hand. I said goodbye. I knew not
how to judge, how to think about judgment. I was a boy again,
mesmerized by the giant, the giant who suddenly had fallen.

Mise-en-Scène

Indigo, aquamarine, turquoise, and a patch
of seafoam: the eye notes it all as we stand
on the sand facing the sea. We always come

back to the sea, its tireless monologue,
the sky above as clear and just as blue.
Between us, few words, the very mark

of familiarity. A quick look suffices,
and we get naked, not an ounce of modesty
between us and no one around to judge us.

In the surf, we are like children again,
yet to be hurt, yet to know hunger or
desperation. We do not bathe; we frolic.

One imagines a ship in the distance, people
on deck with binoculars making out the splash
of water and the movement of our arms,

but nothing like that exists here outside
of our imaginations. The sea god has granted
us an empty beach, an empty slice of the sea,

and clouds as expressive as Impressionists,
clouds revealing the basic shapes: bird, face,
starburst, and tree. The early afternoon ends

with the two of us lying on a single towel,
air-drying so we can dress and return
to the town facing the bay which might as well

be another world. Our arms touch, our hips
touch, and even the air tastes salty at this hour.
We lie there carefully listening to the sea.

Self-Portrait Without a Mirror

It reached a point where I no longer needed
a mirror. I was tired of looking at myself, and I
already knew all of the flaws. Instead of my face,

I just paint a branch of the Japanese plum
in my front yard. My arms now generic
garden hoses. It seems right. I have exhausted

myself. My chest is the state of Maine, and my waist
a cincture from a Catholic priest. I add that for the pure
irony of it. I choose for my left leg the torched arm

of the Statue of Liberty, my right, a Chinese scroll.
I am sure someone will determine some meaning in this,
but I mean to mean absolutely nothing. With age comes

the realization everything departs. My mother once
referred to her particular time in life as the departure
lounge, and I imagined a luxurious airport lounge serving

champagne and carved meats, chocolates and cheeses.
I can't even bother painting just one of these now.
I paint them in sets of twelve, twelve portraits of me

in which there is nothing of me. You want me to give
an explanation. I have none. I have done what I came
to do, and now it is time for me to depart in what

can only be seen as an elegant manner, one devoid
of representation. I will not go to a monastery and sit
still while contemplating nothingness. I took a head start.

Here, my face is that of a lake, and there, a cinnamon bun.
People will have many things to say but, in the end,
let them say I was at least a little bit interesting.

What the God Wishes

From Puerto Morelos, from the shallow cove
with its concrete barrier walls to calm the waters,
the small boat departs. Soon, we are in open sea

sailing toward the Great Mayan Reef that stretches
between the mainland and Cozumel, its deep channels
patrolled by great white sharks. We are deposited

over the reef so as to avoid aforementioned sharks.
For two who believe they came from the sea
and carry within them part of the sea god,

both of us enter the water calmly, as if we had
always been there, the fish swimming by, the rays
ignoring us, the lobsters coming out of rocks to spy.

We are from the sea so we are good swimmers,
and our host relaxes from lifeguard to basic guide.
The sun reflecting against white sand, the water

rocking us in its giant cradle, one feels the god
and his wishes. For the remainder of the day, we are
salty like the sea, taste like the sea, smell like the sea,

salt on our lips, our necks, every inch of us. We do not ask for forgiveness. We do not ask. We lick, we smell, we combine—the sea inside each of us becoming one sea.

The Fountain

Some things are easy to ignore. Take the liver:
it is so incredibly plain. Believe it or not, the ancient
Egyptians were the first to consider it. They chose

to keep birds as a source of food and developed
systems to fatten them by forced feeding. Believe it
or not, we were not the first to dream up ways

to capitalize on the natural world. The French,
as one would guess if taking an examination,
were the ones to refine this forced feeding.

Is there anything the French have not *refined?*
They created guidelines for what they named gavage:
a goose is force-fed three times a day for seventeen days.

Ninety-five days later, the goose is slaughtered,
its liver now transformed into foie gras.
Apparently, there are many steps required

to create luxury. So plain, the ordinary liver.
I say the liver is miraculous, almost mythic.
One can remove 70% of it and the remaining

tissue will regenerate the entirety of the organ.
Can the brain do that? No. I am thinking
about the liver today because I sometimes like to

examine things others overlook. It is a kind of fetish.
The liver makes proteins, removes toxins from our blood.
It is a goddamned hardworking organ.

So today I praise it, I thank it, I relish it. I wish I had
paid more attention to it. As a young man
in Gross Anatomy, I spent a week studying

and dissecting the heart. But we were given
very little time to remove the liver, catalog its
different lobes, and detail its blood supply.

Herodotus introduced us to the concept
of the Fountain of Youth. And for centuries, men
dreamed of finding it. But it was there

within us the entire time. The liver. Examine
any nonagenarian and you will find they all have
highly-functioning livers capable of removing

the poisons produced by life. It turns out
the chemistry of living, the byproducts of living,
are the very things that eventually kill us.

Demigod

Long before the Greeks named him Poseidon,
the Taíno knew his real name was Yúcahu.
And unlike the Greeks and Romans who

chose a belligerent sky god hurling thunderbolts
as somehow superior, the Taíno preferred
to value life over war and its resulting power.

Off the coast, dolphins scissor the surface
and gulls wheel through the air on drafts
unseen save for the birds' turbulent movements.

The sunlight is clean and clear, charged as it is
with ions liberated by the sea. The Taíno word
for salt and seawater is the same: Gua.

And the word for land by the sea is Car,
which made it into English as Cay or Key.
Combine the two and you get Guacar,

twin of Yúcahu and god of the land and harvest.
I spend time thinking through words because
that is what I do. And what some see as brujería,

I see as the magic inherently left to us by the gods.
Some say the gods have abandoned us, and others
say they left parts of themselves behind

in what we may regard merely as other human beings.
In comics, they call these people demigods,
but being half god only makes you more human.

The Taíno believed demigods exist so
the gods can touch us in a more personal way.
And what the Hindus see as reincarnation,

the Taíno see as simply the demigod returning.
The sun at its zenith, the shadows skewed now
and faltering, I cool off in the sea. You think what

I have said is mystical crap, but there are always
truths hidden in plain view. A human body
is 0.4% salt by body weight, a concentration

equivalent to that in seawater. Imagine.
Now do you understand why the Taíno chose
a sea god over all others? They understood he

resides within us all, that our bodies hold
not sky, not wind, not lightning, but the sea.

Blue Moon

It is easy to believe there are no flowers
growing in the folds of sand stretching before us.
Night has erased them. And the blue moon
does little to illuminate anything but the sand:

blue moon, bluish sky, the sand appearing
almost like the sea as it ripples away from us
toward the mountains, like the sea seen at night
from a distance, from a dimly-lit coastal town.

I tell you there are so many things hidden
in this world, and I suspect you know it is true:
flowers, the bay in Tenerife that, despite
its turquoise color, vanishes at night easily.

So many examples, things we know are there
because we have been trained to see them.
When my friend in New York calls to tell me
a new associate, maybe thirty, reminds him of me,

tells me he has the same crooked smile I do
and even my "penguin walk," I laugh about
coincidences. I ask if his name is Alejandro,
and he says it is Alex but could be short for that.

So many hidden things, hidden despite the fact
they are clearly visible. Did I tell the truth? No. No,
I didn't. That truth has been hidden so long my tongue
could not find the words. Even they had vanished.

The man who looks like me, smiles like me,
and walks like me, his skin just a shade lighter than mine,
was born in 1991. I know exactly where he went to school.
I know quite a bit about him, have dreamed of him

for most of my life, even before I knew he existed.
Have I been trained to see him? Not exactly.
The desert so quiet I want to scream, I keep
the silence the way I did when my friend laughed

on the phone about coincidences. I choose not to say
he is my lost but not forgotten son. The blue moon
could not keep him hidden from me the way it does
these flowers. Nothing keeps him hidden from me.

Lustre

They say you lose track of time, and so
I cannot tell how long I have
dipped my hands in this river that promises
a shimmering of gold. I dip my hands
and filter the moving current finding only
rocks, small fish, and detritus. We know
there is not an ounce of gold to be found.
So why do I persist? Why do I stand
knee-deep in the cascading river searching?
You know we get stuck in routines, the wind
and sky changing while we do not. I first
entered the river to help someone I believed
was drowning. Some might see this
as admirable, but it is not. My grandmother
once said intent is almost more important
than action, that good can stem from
bad intent. And so, trust me when I say
this desire was not admirable. I thought
he was drowning, but he was just swimming,
his cries those of simple happiness.
Always trying to save someone: you see?
I was still a child when I first understood
helplessness, the powerful need for someone
to save me. There was no river. There was no gold.

I stood under the water in the shower and felt
my heart inside my chest beating and beating
its distress signal. No one came to save me.
It was a terrible lesson. Up over the ridge
is a smaller bluff that looks out over a sea
of pine and cypress. The view is one many
call beautiful, the world still capable of surprising
even the coldest heart. I choose the easy hike up.
I go easy on myself. I stand and stare out at
that distance. There, one sees on and on
toward the horizon and the ocean we know
is there waiting. I go back to the river often.
No man to save. No gold to find. Once, as a
young man, I learned the power of hunger,
the strength of desperation. I had no choice
but to do what I did. One does not understand
the need to survive until placed in such situations.
I gave up. I gave in. And once again, I prayed
someone would save me. I lay awake at night praying.
I prayed so hard my head hurt, my hands hurt.
Surely someone with good intentions would come
to my rescue. But, no, I rose. I picked the sad
and destroyed version of myself up
and carried him away. I had no other choice.

Sometimes one needs an angel, and sometimes one
needs to be the angel. Go easy on me, my love.
Go easy on me. Yesterday, the City shimmered
in the spring light diffused by the salted air
over the Bay. It was a different kind of beauty,
one made by man but augmented by nature.
There is no gold in the river that I have been
washing my hands in forever. Do you understand
now? Someone has to be the angel. Someone has to
leave the banks and enter the river. Some of us
were never meant to be saved but are asked,
instead, to be the saviors. I save, and I save,
and I save. Again and again, I enter the river, my love.
None of this has ever been about gold.

Oranges

It is difficult, sometimes, to face facts:
you know this. Our parents taught us
to ignore problems, to look away,
and I am no different. I, too, have

needed love so badly I ignored
what was right before my eyes. In the market,
this morning, the oranges were as bright
as little suns radiating their own light.

As a boy, how I admired the way a tree
could blossom and then fill itself with fruit.
I have written about this, chose to look carefully.
But I couldn't turn such focus on myself or,

better yet, on those I chose to love.
When the clerk asked me if I loved oranges,
I said No. And he smiled an uncomfortable smile
as he packed my bags. I paid for my things

and walked home. Twice, I have loved men
who loved alcohol more than they loved
me. Just a fact. I can say it now as fact.
Some say fear fuels these things, fear of

being alone, dying alone. But when are we
not alone? I stood in my kitchen by myself
and unpacked the groceries and thought again
of the clerk's strange smile, the way he

looked at me. There at the bottom of the grocery bag,
a half-dozen oranges. I had forgotten I had them
when he asked me the question. I had forgotten.
The clouds above the Pacific are a soft orange now

as the last light of sunset reflects from beyond
the horizon. I will have oranges after dinner,
the taste as sweet as innocence, what childhood
offered up that was then abruptly taken away.

The Beautiful

In the less turbulent waters found near the river's
bank, in the dark shallows of the Styx, she lowered
her son and waited for his small body to be infiltrated
by the sea god she knew was there, the river touching
the sea after all. It begins this way, the mortal body

forcibly made more divine, made to become half.
Thetis could not bear the fact her union brought forth
an ordinary child, so steps had to be taken,
the infant fortified to become almost a god.
Demigod, they say, with emphasis on the "god."

But we all know that half never receives the same
rights, is never seen as one thing or the other, the child
living out his life as neither. You may as well just
say it, just use the awful term others do: *halfbreed*.
Half. The child should have been at least half,

his mother a Nereid, a sea nymph, a goddess.
But the child entered the world without the glow
the gods can see in each other. For Thetis, this situation
was one she determined to overcome by whatever means,
no matter the cost. She could not afford an ordinary son.

She made the mistake we all know well,
held onto her son by his heel for fear he be swept
downriver, held on as she dipped him in waters
that swallowed all light as if an ink. She held on,
granting him the sole spot that rendered him mortal.

Do not pity the man named Achilles. Do not lament
the fact an arrow caught him in his vulnerable heel.
I say there is a quiet beauty in mortality, and one should
not pity the beautiful. Pity Patroclus, instead, the ungodly
man who bruised Achilles's heart and left it burning.

Moonlit Elegy

The moonlight made the sand shine softly,
and we sat side by side, our shoulders touching,
two seventeen-year-old boys who wanted

to be men. Palm fronds whispered as they
caught the breeze coming in from the ocean,
as if they needed to be part of the conversation.

It was late, and there were few if any people
on the beach, and it only took a compliment,
a you-are-so-handsome, to get me to kiss you.

And so it began, so a friendship that should never
have happened began. For decades, our friendship
lived on and on through laughter and arguments,

through sadness and moments of exquisite joy.
How I wish I could step back in time and end
our last phone call differently. How I wish I could

have shown my annoyance without showing
cruelty. A day later you were gone, the car accident
resulting in a broken windshield that sliced

your chest open. I still dream of this. Even last night,
I dreamt it, the glass, the slice, the ungodly
amounts of blood. I could not protect you; I

never could. And my opportunity to apologize
was erased more quickly than my anger was.
I promised myself I would not write any elegies

for my next book, and here I am writing an elegy.
But it is the least I can do. It is the least I can do for you.
In our long game of friendship, you always said

I was the strong one. But am I? Does a strong man
hold anger above friendship? Does he turn
his back when times are tough? I don't think so.

This man is weak. This man stands here saying he is
sorry, so sorry, forgive me. He says I love you,
so much so he cannot yet use the past tense.

The Nipple Fish

Believe me, I know these fish. They are no joke.
The Cenote Cristalino appears as if it has captured
the sky above and liquefied it, and in the heat

of late afternoon, it appears even more seductive
than it normally does. But then there are the fish,
the nipple fish, tiny fish that, for whatever reason,

like to nip at the nipples. I tell the truth here.
And as we enter the waters of the cenote,
the very minute the water is above the nipple line,

we feel them. Not painful, but definitely surprising.
What is the lesson here? Must there always be a lesson?
Even the most beautiful places carry something less

than beautiful? I don't know, but we both laugh
as the fish pay us attention that we weren't expecting.
The sun tilts and tilts, and the shadows begin creating

even darker blues among the bright ones that drew
us here in the first place. We swim and marvel.
We keep moving to avoid the surprise of these fish

that are always just waiting, waiting for you to stop
moving so they can remind you why their name is so apt.
For a couple of long hours, we swim in the sky.

We are like gods who have returned to the heavens,
to the seas, but the bites from tiny fish in these waters
remind us we remain human, all too human.

The Checklist

You have checked and double-checked. You have
gone through each step and every permutation
even as you stand in the shower. But somehow,
despite that, you haven't had the success you expected.

When you have to tell someone that the treatment
has failed, when your voice softens and you can
barely get the words out; when the person asks
what that means, what can we do now, what

are you saying to me, you try your best to be calm.
Because what it means is often that the cancer
can no longer be controlled. And to say that, to put
the words into the air, is something no one wants.

Often, you are met with tears but, sometimes, anger.
One cannot predict the emotions that will be brought
to the surface, or the speed at which they will erupt.
And you can say we all come to that time, but it is

different when that time is staring you down.
I sit. I speak slowly. I try my best not to cry because
the doctor crying is never perceived as remotely helpful.
I sit. I listen. I offer whatever I can to be somewhat reassuring.

Outside the hospital, I am always careful, always watchful when driving out to head home. The hospital is a place of great stress, of great emotions, and people are often arriving or departing carelessly. You have to be watchful.

When the student asks again how to do it, how to break the news, I tell her to trust her own gut, to trust the cues between herself and the patient. She wants a guide, a checklist, but nothing like that exists. It has never existed.

Blue on Blue

Cap de Ses Salines, Mallorca

Mirror, mirror: the sea and sky here are one,
the varying shades of blue reflecting back
and forth so slowly they are virtually unseen.

The sea god Yúcahu, the one inside the two of us
since just after we were born, the god that called
us to each other, calls us now to enter the sea.

And we strip down—without modesty or shame—
on the virgin beach. We comply; we enter
the water from which the better part of us came.

When we touch in the sea, there are no shootings,
no killings, not even the awfulness of politics. We are
as we were made, and for a moment it feels like innocence.

I count seven shades of blue around us not including
what rises from the horizon and becomes the largest
of skies. And when we return to the shore, we lie

and stare at the sea as if hypnotized. Neither can ignore
the god before us, the same one who swims within us.
The lighthouse in the distance keeps its watch.

The sargassum inks the edge of the shoreline.
And here under this sky, we lie side by side.
We are each other's home, and we do not deserve

the dark world we know exists outside of this place.
Always and at any time, someone is dying. Someone
is happier than they have ever been. The sea god knows

what is his, and for those hours we lie together
on the sand looking at each other with eyes as if to say:
Stay here, stay with me, let us never leave this place.

from *The Day Underneath the Day* (2001)

Homage to William Carlos Williams

I   *The Body*

       You removed integument.
You palpated red fibrils,
       extracted breastplates,
exposed diaphragms.
       You saw the once rhythmic heart
still silent, again and again, in a pool of formalin.

       We begin the study of life
with our hands buried in the dead.
       This is how you did it
and how we will always do it.
       The body refuses the name *body*,
taking *cadaver*, meaning *to fall*.

II   *Corpus*

Nothing could keep you away.
Not *Histology*. Not *Gray's Anatomy*.
You filled the margins of *Physiology*

with notes for poems.
Nothing could keep you away.
Not surgery. Not psychiatry. Not pediatrics.

Not the blankness of corridors.
Not the doctors you called teacher.
Not the New Jersey days silenced by snow.

Nothing could keep you away.
Not the little girl bundled against the winter sunlight.
Not the yellow wheelbarrow outside her window.

III   *The Body in Bloom*

Geneva, the Lycée Condorcet in Paris,
the snow erasing everything . . .
how easily you forgot
the scholastic virtue of traveling.
You did not question the lizards

that ate contradictions
—both flies and flower buds—
the way *corpus* encompassed
not only art but the body
silent in the morgue.

You did not question
the truth of liver,
the truth of lungs,
the truth of blood when we are cut
so the body blooms.

The Field

The hum of wood-lice,
the way it
approximates

the frequency of C$^{\#}$,
the way it is heard
only in close

proximity
to the rotting tree
that stands alone

in the field;
the wildflowers,
their colors, the fact

they are nothing
but weeds, their leaves
prickly like weeds;

the grasses, greens
easily separated
by the trained eye

into celadon, civette,
patina, veronese, reseda,
the common leaf green

or shoe-bottom mold;
only with such detail
do I love you—

the paper-thin curls of bark
on our shirts, the dry grass
falling from our hair

Minutiae

Even now, whole patches of grass,
still white without moonlight,
testify that yes, the fire
consumed everything, laid down

white ash to mark its territory.
The sky is blue; the grass, white.
How else should I begin?
Should I begin with the walls

of the church, crumbled
under the weight of the flames?
Should I begin with the stained glass
now a spiculated pool of amethyst

come to rest against a metal beam?
Begin with the absent crucifix
or the tabernacle door wide open?
No. To begin is to start from zero.

Only then can we layer minutiae
upon minutiae, the whole picture
rising from the details, careful or not.
And so I tell you that there

among the rubble, feet away
from the ashen grass, I saw a vine
(well, a vine-like, weedy plant) growing,
pushing its small red petals into the air.

South Beach

Memory brings us back to such a place—
the rows of photinia, each leaf a red flame
(blood-tinged, almost) violent in sunlight,
the sand not the white of the Caribbean

but the dingy mud-grey of south Florida,
the Atlantic sluicing the reef, whitening it
for seconds at a time, the sea sifting
through porous rock, patiently erasing it.

In a pool of standing water, clouds.
On the rocks, the sunlight on our backs,
you are looking into a puddle instead of
looking at the sea, its upside-down *V*'s

advancing. Curious, I look as well.
According to the physics of wind on water,
our faces wrinkle. I see my lips saying:
I will love you, I have always loved you.

On Privilege

The rampant cane fields rife with disease,
the ocean carrying only shells to the altar,
a beach left to penitents, their easy sweat
cursing the sand that brought an increase
in tourism. Could this scene be altered?

Next to a pile of seaweed, the ubiquitous gull
ate from a plate of dead things, rejections.
Up in the cane fields, sitting beside an anthill,
a young and foolish version of myself had once hid,
scratching in the dirt his tired testament, his will.

To my firstborn, I would leave the sea; the sand,
to my future love. But my father's grim shovel
I would bury under a palm tree, under tendrils
of clematis, its showy blooms filled with poisons.
One should not be alone in the cane fields, its evil

captured in its wide paragraphs, its evil refined
like sugar. At a resort staggered down a cliff side
to yet another beach, I sat one morning studying
the flowers of the crown-of-thorns, its bloodletting
worthy of an entire chapter in a book

on phlebotomy. In the air, I smelled privilege.
I remembered the cane fields. The years rewind
so easily for one who is a visitor in his own home.
The sea silences these false lines and mocks me
with promises of splendor and bright fish, reminds me

I am a fisherman, casting an empty hook.

Arripare

Discovery Bay, Jamaica

Under this cloudless sky, the sea is more blue
than green, the light binding to the salt air
with the force of molecular physics.

Surely Ixfœtay understood this,
Ixfœtay who watched the sea and sky
to warn his tribe about storms,

Ixfœtay, called son of the sea in Arawak,
Ixfœtay, the man who discovered, supposedly,
that bauxite mixed with water could be used as ink.

Ixfœtay. I spell your name incorrectly,
the way Colón spelled it
in his logs filled with clouds and small Latin.

You must not have been well that day.
You must have stayed home while your wives
counted the coconuts, the guavas, the children.

Did you believe you could forecast
by the sky alone, that the clouds
were wiser than all the watchers before you?

Where were you that day?
Why were you not at the bay staring at the horizon,
you who had done so for twelve years?

Just so, a red cross, billowing in the wind,
rose from the horizon and entered the bay
under a sky that betrayed no storm.

from *The Second Person* (2007)

Night Air

"If God is Art, then what do we make
of Jasper Johns?" One never knows
what sort of question a patient will pose,

or how exactly one should answer.
Outside the window, snow on snow
began to answer the ground below

with nothing more than foolish questions.
We were no different. I asked again:
"Professor, have we eased the pain?"

Eventually, he'd answer me with:
"Tell me, young man, whom do you love?"
"E," I'd say, "None of the Above,"

and laugh for lack of something more
to add. For days he had played that game,
and day after day I avoided your name

by instinct. I never told him how
we often wear each other's clothes—
we aren't what many presuppose.

Call it an act of omission, my love.
Tonight, while walking to the car,
I said your name to the evening star,

clearly pronouncing the syllables
to see your name dissipate
in the air, evaporate.

Only the night air carries your words
up to the dead (the ancients wrote):
I watched them rise, become remote.

Currency

Wind fingering the sea-grass at the edge
of the dune, and again, in the distance,
darkness of rain coming from the West.

But to use the word *coming* is imprecise—
the rain spreads like a bruise over the ocean,
lingers and advances with terrible accuracy.

So, too, sadness is seen approaching.
One smells it, the characteristic ozone
old women use to predict inclement weather.

Is there anything as universal as sadness?
The mist sifts through the avenues
without lightning or the crack of thunder;

drifts past the windows, surprising no one;
swirls through the slats of the fire escape
down past the neighbors' grimy windows.

Once, I bought a man's attention at a bar
with the currency of sadness: the ocean
and its ink-dark swells challenging

the cliff side; the draft whistling through
windowpanes; a darkening slice of the moon—
I give unto Caesar what is Caesar's.

Sotto Voce

The humidity, somewhere around 95%,
simply would not allow the steam to lift
in generous curls from the street that day.

Instead, a dirty pool lay in the center
of the intersection, something dark
at the crossroads. Any minute,

some half-naked Augustine would take his place
center stage, dripping with spray-bottle sweat,
his right fist beating his chest:

Mea culpa, Mea culpa, Mea culpa.
Afternoons so slow in their departure
simply begged to be entertained, and so

my friend and I rolled around in bed, fully clothed,
mimicking one of a dozen sordid scenes:
always the imitations, the assignments

to be fulfilled—each verb precise, each
adverb filled with practiced lust—
our sin rehearsed until it was flawless.

Maelstrom

Wind shook the trees and rain crackled
at the windows. Could it have been
any other way? Rain coming down,
clothes wet, water dripping from our hair?

At the window, could it have been
a ghost singing its final warning?
Clothes wet, water dripping from our hair,
he fell on me like rain. I could not speak.

A ghost sang its final warning
like a storm. He tore my shirt open
and fell on me like rain. I could not speak,
and I closed my eyes. It started like this.

Like a storm, he tore my shirt open,
the light in the stairwell flickering
as I closed my eyes. It started like this:
the steps pressing into my back,

the light in the stairwell flickering
sensing storm, our hands trembling.
The steps pressed into my back
under the sound of belts unbuckling.

Sensing storm, our hands trembled.
I could not watch, could not speak.
Under the sound of belts unbuckling,
a future unraveled like spun gold.

I could not watch, could not speak
then. And now, years later, the same
future unravels like spun gold:
the arguments, the body's betrayals.

Then and now, years later, the same
quiet lying about the house.
The arguments, the body's betrayals
resist closure or the quick dismissal.

This quiet lies about my house.
Again wind shakes the trees and rain crackles.
You resist closure or the quick dismissal.
Rain coming down. It started like this.

Influence

Not even fever can conjure the stars
above Florence just before sunrise.
Yet we know that centuries ago it did,

or maybe it was the other way around.
Mrs. X, we were told, died
in severe respiratory distress.

The pathologist, our teacher (Mrs. X's
lungs in his hands), mumbled something
about the influence of the stars.

I will not attempt to imitate his accent.
He is from somewhere in Eastern Europe,
somewhere where they *really* like black bread,

even late in the evening before bed;
this, and more, he had mentioned before.
But Mrs. X, her lungs consolidated, dusky,

hemorrhagic, was our true lesson that day,
dare we forget the purpose of our studies.
Given a minor portion of her history,

a chance to examine her lungs thoroughly,
not one of us made the correct diagnosis.
And so, we were dismissed,

given one hour, a luxury we were told,
to ascertain the true cause of demise.
Seated at the microscope, we examined,

one after another, Mrs. X's slides, each
of us noting the classic cytoplasmic inclusions,
the overwhelming inflammation.

Only then did we understand what our teacher
understood long before looking under a microscope—
Influenza: under the gravest influence of the stars.

Invective

From the Turnpike, north-central Florida,
the body in transit can sight a red dirt road
climbing a small hill, and yes, it cannot help
but note the final turn before that road

vanishes in skyline and emptiness.
There in the car, another lesson in vantage.

What next? A lesson about the weather?
The impending front? Abstraction was coming,
and the signs along the road said to make ready,
start now, repent. But not even abstraction

could have stopped what was already happening:
red the dirt road in Florida, red the bauxite-laden

dirt of Mandeville, fifty years earlier, my father
walking up a hill utterly unimpressed
with the red earth there beneath his feet.
Had I, too, been conditioned? Hardened?

Every patient in my study died in two years,
and what had I done, presented the facts

at a conference, answered questions
about protocols and confidence intervals?
I used to tell the dead about dying.
Now I search for crude metaphors, like this dirt.

Σ

The symbol with the sharpest edges
and the power to sum an infinite
number of variables, the one

that allows the common 1
to stand not only side by side
with the mysteries of X and Y

and the likes of that oh-so-elusive π
but links them and makes them more
as if to remind us it is

the only one-symbol formula which,
when translated from arithmetic,
means not just summation

but melting pot, or better yet,
all-inclusive (with an exclamation mark).
Even now, I do not understand

the workings of Σ. What I do know
is that many years ago a woman
sat up in bed and died. In the days

since her accident, a thrombus had grown
deep in her thigh, grew until it broke free
and traveled through her veins, her heart,

to lodge in her pulmonary artery.
Our attending physician, our teacher,
had asked us how we might prevent such a thing.

He prodded us, suggested we use all
we had learned so far in medical school—
Until then, Σ had never seemed so important.

August

I   On the Corner of Fourth & Irving

Fog instead of twilight, and the pigeons
scattering into the air. The ground tremors
with the weight of an oncoming streetcar.

For a minute the air is a blur of wings,
the sound of wings, reflections of wings
like madness in the windows across the street.

Black street. Grey sky. Waning light illuminates
the fog. One wants to call it ghostly, but does not:
I had read his chest x-ray as negative.

The fog coming in quickly now, blown
uphill from the Pacific, the air stirring
the inanimate scraps on the sidewalk.

Eight out of ten people with this cancer
are cured five years after receiving radiation.
Wrong streetcar. The temperature falling.

The pigeons landing and then taking flight.
What if we, too, had hollow bones?
Today, the x-ray showed a mass, the tumor

there again in the center of his chest.
I am tired of standing here clutching textbooks,
the pigeons circling overhead afraid to land.

II To Marie Curie

Fog instead of twilight, and the pigeons
clustering along the edges of rooftops.
In that light, Paris was not Paris.

The laboratory was not yet a monument
to Science. There, in the last light,
the radium portioned out, your fingers

already slender, you held a small sample
with a makeshift forceps, like this.
Decay. The expulsion of particles. Radium.

Radium, which when held too long
caused skin ulcers, caused tumors to shrink.
Madame Curie, you would be surprised to see

what we have done with your discovery.
Today, we fire electrons into metal,
the resulting radiation barreling into the body.

Today, I felt lymph nodes in the young man's neck,
much larger than they were five years ago
when they might have been a ghost on an x-ray.

I have failed. He has not been cured.
The wind erases the sounds on the street—
only the beating and beating of wings.

The Tree Frog

It is not the chambers of the heart that hold him
captive, but the hallways of the mind. Why
his image burning green and blue persists
—the face, the eyes questioning, the shape
of his head—is beyond anything I can understand.

What lessons must be learned to overcome
the final act of longing? This morning, sunlight
grasped at everything, but the wind swept
through the streets taking things with it,
even the soul. Sometimes the curtain does not

completely fall, and the play, barely visible,
continues. This much I know. This much
the textbooks have taught us. The blind man
Cervantes built continued to see and saw far
too much, could not accept the utter purity

of Abstraction. But is that not our essential fault?
A tree frog croaks against the backdrop of memory,
and the cold sheets and darkened room return,
but you are not here to whisper me to sleep.
The ocean's long-windedness offers no replacement

for your voice, anxious the way it could be at night.
What is there to understand? Not the heart, certainly
not the heart that is so easily trained to forget.
Night after night, like the tree frog, I remind myself
who I am, voicing what I cannot voice during the day.

Proximity

I have forgotten my skin, misplaced my body.
Tricks of mind, a teacher once said: the man
with the amputated right arm convinced he could

feel the sheets and air-conditioned air touching
the phantom skin. There must be a syndrome
for such a thing, a named constellation of symptoms

that correspond to the ghost hand and what it senses.
This morning, I felt your hand touch me on the shoulder
the way you would when you turned over in your sleep.

What syndrome describes this? Not the sense of touch
but of being touched. Waking, I felt my own body,
piece by piece, dissolving: my hands, finger by finger,

then the legs and the chest leaving the heart exposed
and beating, the traveling pulses of blood
expanding the great vessels. The rib cage vanished

and then the spine. If your right hand offends you,
wrote Mark, cut it off and throw it away,
for it is better for you to lose a part than to lose

the whole. But I have no word for this phantom
touch, and the fully real feeling of the hair
on your arm shifting over my own as your hand

moved from my shoulder and out across my chest.
Desire makes me weak, crooned the diva,
or was it Augustine faced with his own flesh?

Whisper me a few lies, god, beautiful and familiar lies.

The Sad Name Enters the Room

What manner of dream or of rapture
allows the body to betray the mind like this?
At the first performance of Berlioz' *Requiem*,
in the crisis of the *Tuba Mirum*, the often solemn

priests had to be removed from the hall,
their tears surprising their own faces.
But the body often betrays the mind,
the hand moving where it knows it shouldn't,

the eye wandering out past the horizon
of another person's smile.
Who can confess to understanding such things?
Dark of night, the body climbing into the waking,

my mouth opening, my voice asking that the arm
be removed from my chest. But how is it
another man's name slips from my mouth,
even then when the mind should have learned better?

In the darkest of night, in the bed where I
have been resting, the sad name enters the room
via my own mouth. And the arm responds,
moves from my chest, moves back toward

the loved one lying faithfully beside me
without even the slightest recognition of my error.
Sometimes the body cannot be held in check:
the slip of the tongue, the wandering hand....

Years ago, in the darkened lecture hall of Medicine,
slides documenting many kinds of pathology,
my Professor pronounced: there is nothing filthier
than the recesses of the human mouth.

The Tunnel

I had been there before, of course, the air
still faintly smelling of smoke. Three dollars
to ride, to navigate the currents of Love,

the crests and slurries of opportunity sold as easily
as cotton candy or a soda, as easily as my heart.
O god of Free Enterprise. O winged child

smiling from the placard with your arrow
set to fly. Which couple did you choose that night?
The boat motored ahead, its track sunken

but there to offer safe passage through rough times.
I clasped the edge of his flannel shirt, warmer
and different from the silk one I had held on to

so many years ago as the sulfur flames fanned out
above our heads. The mirrors showed our faces
silvered in that flash, my hair almost white

with surprise. What called us to such things?
What drew us into that boat without a ferryman?
A goddess whispered that all would be seen

and foreseen along Love's tides and riptides.
At the end of that journey, we walked out
under a sky bleeding pink and orange. And then,

it darkened with birdsong and so many possibilities.
Make me a candle, Lord. Make me less blue.
Make me faithful, something tried but true.

Cri de cœur

The trees are dark and heavy, my love,
heavy with the sound of the locust—
the dead of summer has arrived.

The lane scripts its old questions
carefully down a canyon of trees.
Green, the sunlight shifts

and dims the credibility of things,
and then the pond is a field,
weedy and green, weedy;

the hospital, dirty squares of light
against a background of trees
dark with the sound of the locust.

Sleeping god in an age of plagues,
give us the chance to use the past tense.
Let us, with the charity of middle age, lie:

"Yes, it was all so beautiful. . ."

from *Torn* (2011)

Windows

Who ever knew that light could be so blue—
not even the light traversing the windows
in Beacon Hill was ever so blue, the once

translucent glass brought from Italy
transformed by Boston weather into the sickly
blue of blue-bloods. There is a story to be told.

Today, the blue water goblet is all that remains
of that history. And blue is its own story. Here,
in such blue light, I am the falling man, and you

the purpled dove, and you the six-edged star
that is brilliant but not bright. It is said
the most difficult things to paint are one's hands

or eyes. Yours have a speck of light in the right
upper quadrant of the iris and four shades of brown,
the darkest at the outermost edge; and yours,

lit up and sparkling with the reflections
of the jeweled chandelier dangling overhead.
The story isn't a difficult one to start, the way

a painter, after collecting many images,
approaches the canvas with something akin
to longing or need. How Rembrandt

understood so clearly the darkest quality
of our eyes is beyond us. But there is much
we will never understand. Darkness is its own

sad story. And mine? It begins like this:
Listen, outside there are two great trees,
their branches wild, twisted, and twisting . . .

La Revancha del Tango

In my mouth, song. In my ear, your own song:
so much amor, this dance… The chin cocked

to facilitate a side-long glance, the arch
of the back, the quick spark of Santa Maria

that races from thigh to knee to ball of the foot,
the stamp, that singular sound, the sound

of *you-will-have-me-tonight*. Arch
of the back, the return of your body

to mine. Spanish guitar, the slicked-back
black hair, and Santa Maria of the evening

who invites all that is forbidden in public:
the hand on shoulder, the hand on back,

on waist, the perspiration a glue
between curve of hand and the curve

of the neck. Santa Maria of Argentina, I pray
to you, to this beautiful man who follows

my lead. No flowers, no rose in my teeth.
I carry only song in my mouth.

What some call lust, others call *the calculation*.
We were fooled by the Virgin, by the music's

instructions to love. Santa Maria of Argentina,
flower behind her ear, the mouth about to sing

the song of laughter. Virgin-goddess, necessary whore—
There is, indeed, a subtle logic to seduction.

The Kiss

If $E=mc^2$, then how fast is my mind moving right now?
Follow me: there is a boy in the cane fields
praying not to be found. It is not the father's belt—
no, that is only a small source of fear—but the other

boys that frighten him, the boys who beat him, kick him.
And then, as if to puzzle, the biggest of them will hold
him down, kiss him, the bully's hands unbuckling
belts. In this, children are no different.

Anything else in the world seems better
than this image, these boys. Schoolyard, noontime,
the clearing just beyond the wide expanse of cane,
the shallow caves down by the seaside.

Follow me: can words really hurt? Do actions
speak louder? *Sissy, homo, faggot.* Could these
be real ammunition? There is a beach in Ibiza,
not a cane field in sight. There, in the early evening,

I saw a man bend slowly to kiss another man.
I assumed they were lovers. I assumed they
had known each other for many years
or had met at a bar earlier that afternoon.

The young Italian who had been kissed rose
and walked along the shore toward me. As he passed,
I told him it was beautiful, that kiss. But the mind
is never fast enough, you see. It is never fast enough.

The eyes saw what they wanted to see, saw tenderness.
But there was nothing like that there. The kiss?
It had been a warning. The kiss meant *change your ways
or risk harm.* Brutish, that tenderness. Sharp, too.

Blood

Someone has already pulled a knife
across my chest, and the rope has already
gripped our wrists drawing blood.

I am naked, and I cannot be sure
if you are as well. In the room, the men
come and go, yelling *blood bath*, *half-blood*,

blood-bitch. We never hear the word *trueblood*.
In my dreams I am dying all the time.
We are bound and gagged, blindfolded,

but still I know you must be the one
lying there, the cool anodized steel table
beneath us, the two of us side by side.

Lying there, my shoulder blades ache,
and there is blood collecting in
the corners of my mouth. But then it happens,

just as it always happens: your fingers
suddenly twist into tiny shoots, your arms
break free as you accept the shape

of a tree, the leaves sprouting, the delicate
bark rising up from your skin's surface.
Try as I might, I never seem able.

On the telephone this morning, I again
keep the dream to myself. Half-blood
becomes half-breed. Blood-bitch

becomes blood-sister. But Blood never lies,
does it? Blood carries so many secrets
one can only hear its murmurs in our arteries,

its incessant monologue, in the quiet
night's bed just before sleep. Blood says
You are more and, sometimes, *You are less*.

The Bridge

I love. Wouldn't we all like to start
a poem with "I love…"? I would.
I mean, I love the fact there are parallel lines
in the word "parallel," love how

words sometimes mirror what they mean.
I love mirrors and that stupid tale
about Narcissus. I suppose
there is some Narcissism in that.

You know, Narcissism, what you
remind me to avoid almost all the time.
Yeah, I love Narcissism. I do.
But what I really love is ice cream.

Remember how I told you
no amount of ice cream can survive
a week in my freezer. You didn't believe me,
did you? No, you didn't. But you know now

how true that is. I love
that you know my Achilles heel
is none other than ice cream—
so chilly, so common.

And I love fountain pens. I mean
I just love them. Cleaning them,
filling them with ink, fills me
with a kind of joy, even if joy

is so 1950. I know, no one talks about
joy anymore. It is even more taboo
than love. And so, of course, I love joy.
I love the way joy sounds as it exits

your mouth. You know, the *word* joy.
How joyous is that. It makes me think
of bubbles, chandeliers, dandelions.
I love the way the mind runs

that pathway from bubbles to dandelions.
Yes, I love a lot. And right here,
walking down this street,
I love the way we make

a bridge, a suspension bridge
—almost as beautiful as the
Golden Gate Bridge—swaying
as we walk hand in hand.

Inheritance

Long Dead. He had been *Long Dead.* Such an odd phrase.
How long is *Long Dead*? How many moons is that?
But my use of the words "many moons" offended
my Great Uncle, who raised his eyebrows and mumbled
that I should stop speaking like a pansy. I did not
know then that flowers could speak. I wasn't old enough.
I rehearsed the words in my head, repeating them
with various inflections: many moons, many moons.
And when I tired, I shouted that there was a murder
of crows in the yard. Ah the English sneer, the slight curl
of the upper lip and the flaring of the tight nostrils.
Great Uncle barked something about a gaggle of geese.
When it was pointed out there were no crows in the yard,
oh the looks, the shaking of heads, the word liar
and, again, pansy. Yes, I was alive by the Grace of God.
By the Grace of God: it sounded so lovely, so pristine.
Grace, that beautiful but difficult thing to divine,
and God, well, God was God. The teacup returned
to its saucer so quickly it broke. The book glided,
like the quickest of jaybirds, into the kitchen window.
What had I said? What could I possibly have said?
That William Richard Extant August would have killed me,
that he should have killed my mother, is all I remember
my Great Uncle shouting. I was not a real man, a man's

man, a man of guts, a pure man, an honorable man.
In the portrait of him near the sunroom, his head tilted
between direct stare and a sly, almost feminine, profile,
there was a mole on the upper inner edge of his left earlobe.
William Richard Extant August, I had never met you.
I had never killed anything with my bare hands.
And years later, having learned to shave, I find it.
There, on my ear, the same mole, in the same spot.
Long Dead? No, not dead at all. Asleep. Resting.
Waiting for the right time to make himself known.

Nature

Half-joking, half-serious, seriously halved,
I wanted to find Him in the empty sleeve
of air surrounding the bell's clapper.

Would He not be found there, hovering
in the air prepared to carry sound? So many
silly ideas the adolescent carries around.

So many of us vowed chastity, the easy gesture
for those who had denied their own nature.
But Nature could not be ignored—the way it

snaps the heads off mice, takes the hatchlings
one by one, breaks the mule's back. I understood
the rules. We all did. Rule #1: show kindness

to your brother. I wanted to show more
than kindness, wanted to favor my brothers,
for lack of a better word. Rule #2: Do unto others…

I won't even go there. What point in that now?
There was always God reclining in the empty space
beside my hand, beside the thenar eminence,

beside my careful eyes that imagined the other
boys in all of their happiness. In every man, God
had placed Himself. In every man, I sought

to touch that God. Silly, I know. Silly.
What I wanted then was to break God's heart—
I wanted Him to snap my neck, break my back.

Paying Attention

I know everything about my God.
Can you tell me about your own?

Outside the window, rain. Well, the sound
of rain. Why would I start this way?
Because my God prefers a preamble—
Spool of lightning, Fist of night-blooming jasmine.

My God can slice me clean open from head
to the arches of my feet, does so easily
with a swipe of His index fingernail, a clean
slice to show you the back half of me

seen from the front. He sometimes puts me
back together again. But with my front half
gone, He licks the back wall of my throat,
His tongue like sweetened gasoline.

The sound of rain against my window
is louder than expected, is my God
reminding me to pay attention. And my God
despises inattention and punishes me often

for it. He strips me of my clothes and lashes
my back with his cat-o-nine-tails. I am
quick to cry, so quick to promise humility. I am
a liar. I am weak and a liar. And I am punished.

What more can I tell you? What can I say
to explain my God? He has little tolerance
for hatred. He expects undying love
and affection. He leaves the large red

imprints of his fist against my back,
sometimes flowering on my face. He showers
me with expectations. He lifts me up
to remind of my foolish fear of heights.

Or Something Like That

In the Yard today, the pine needles began snowing
down. The way they caught the light was curious.
And the maple's leaves, all red and ochre, were

already littering the walkway. I, well I sat
thinking the same dark thoughts I have had
since childhood. You know the ones. I need

not explain them to You, of all people.
But it is so easy to call things dark thoughts,
a kind of lazy shorthand. Too easy to forget

the maxim that everyone is good in Your eyes.
We both know this is not true, is a lie. I mean,
the high school counselor they put away for life…

How can he be good in Your eyes? Sometimes,
I am convinced no one is good in Your eyes.
Dark thoughts, yes. I am doubting again.

I doubt the pine needles, the maple leaves,
the robin carrying on its stupid song,
my own voice mumbling on a slate blue terrace.

Easy to doubt. Always easy. And the old Jesuit
who lectured me on this? Well, he doubted, too.
But I am not quite ready to be broken just yet.

I have a few things left in me, a few surprises.
No magic is as good as Your magic, but I have
hidden cards up my sleeve, twisted the handkerchief,

slipped the coin behind my watch. I still have
a few tricks left to play. And the light shifting
on the terrace, the pine needles coming down,

I know what they mean. I get what You are trying
to get at. I am here, God, I am here. I am waiting
for You to blind me with a sunstorm of stars.

In the Cutting Room

That the falling glass, the one
that falls 4 feet before shattering
into 18 pieces, is caught in something
between 64 and an infinite number of frames
between edge of table and the kitchen's

fake Italian marble floor.... This is exactly
the kind of crap I cannot stand to hear.
God in the details. God in the minutiae
of a falling body, a mass falling
through space and time. What shutter fly genius,

what poet of a scientist discovered this?
I reject the scientific. I have
halted the glass exactly 4 inches
above the ground and reveled in the
"potential" of it. I have halted your heart

exactly 4 inches above the ground. See
how easily I revise our history? See how I
have swapped my heart for your own?
The falling heart about to shatter, held
in space, in time, by the mind's quicker-than-thou

apertures? Exactly the kind of crap I cannot stand.
I have held a heart in my own hands, the heavy
rubbery mass of it slick with blood and saline.
With forceps and dissecting probe, I have
opened each valve, studied its small ears

that sometimes fill with blood. Circumflex,
Left Anterior Descending, I have followed
the pathways blood takes around the heart.
I am not qualified to speak about God and Physicks.
I have no gift for the 35-mm world of

quick shutter and quicker thought. Who does?
I speak what I know. I speak with a filthy mouth.
And what do I know? What could I possibly know?
That the heart is tougher than you think. That it
does not break. That it, too, becomes dust.

Corpus Medicum

In the dream of fever, in the murky light
of a mind ill-at-ease, it is the tile I remember,
the single row of beige tile that circumnavigated

the laboratory, a tile that seemed more in keeping
with a bathroom decorated in the 1970's
than with a room in which to dissect cadavers.

Below the tile, a lime-like pale green, and above,
the clean white of hospitals. In the dream of fever,
I am there again in the first days trying to speak

the dead language of naming: *latissimus, pectoralis,*
orbicularis orbis. For some of us, this was a language
we had heard before we could comprehend

the alpha and omega of *muscularis.* Someone
whispered that the very act of naming was holy.
Cingularum that became *cingulare*, the cincture

that held the cassock in place. But fever
brings much more than the simple images
of the past, brings with it the smell of the sacristy

and His Reverence standing still
as one of us undid the cincture at his waist.
O black cassock, weren't we the lucky ones,

the special boys who were allowed into the secret
rooms of the Church? In the anatomy laboratory,
my head lowered and intent on study, the smell

was anything but human—the smell of formalin
and bleach disguised the glistening corpus,
disguised the human stench. And had I not seen this

attempt at deception before, seen it as a child
when our dirty hands and mouths were covered,
all hushed by the language of Rome and perfumed

by the incense left clinging to Monsignor's large hands?
Out of one dead language another one rose easily.
Cingularum that became *cingulare*, cincture that became a cinch.

Imprimatur

The ones who paint the word *Latino* on my forehead
think me lazy and careless. The ones who pin
Asian-American to my chest consider me a hard worker.

Unfortunately, the Pulmonologist charged with
inspiring us with the tradition of the physical exam
felt I belonged to the former. You hear people

sometimes ask for a definition of cruelty
because you know they have never tried imagining
a life other than their own. And the definitions,

every last one, are pointless. Cruelty, of what we
are all capable. *See one, do one, teach one,*
we are told repeatedly. And after having seen

my teacher place a central line twice, he demands
I jump in and place the line this woman needs.
Her veins had collapsed. I watched her watch

my hands shaking. And I could see that she saw
something like terror in my face. I am focusing
so hard on the skin near the clavicle that I can

almost count the pores there. The bore in my hand.
The pressure to break the skin greater than I thought.
And when I miss the vessel, when the needle slips

into a different space, air suddenly starts spewing
back at me from the needle's slim body, the air
a tiny whistling sound. And I see the muscles

in her neck starting to flex more, trying
to compensate for the sudden diminishment of oxygen
as her right lung collapses. I am too scared to cry.

And the Pulmonologist is mumbling something
about how I now get to learn a different procedure.
He is saying something about placing a chest tube,

about re-expanding her dropped lung.
But I am not paying attention, cannot pay attention,
the woman's face, her eyes, the calmness

with which she looks at me and says that it
will be okay, that she will be fine. And when
my teacher punctures the skin and muscles between

her ribs, when the blood begins to trickle slowly
across her side, I freeze. I cannot get myself
to shove the tube into the newly made hole.

And I am lazy. I am a lazy spic, my teacher says,
his anger visible in the quickness with which he places
the tube in her chest. And when the tears start

clouding my eyes, he tells me to keep my mouth shut,
that this procedure is straightforward, is black
or white. I can barely breathe. Surely my own lungs

are collapsing. And there is anger in his voice.
The world of Medicine is black or white, he says.
And I am worried. And all I can think about

is the cru in cruelty, that cross, that crux,
and the black or white world of Medicine,
a world in which I do not even exist.

The Personal

Wear the wedding ring on a chain around your neck.
The personal, as in personal life? Say nothing.
This is how I spoke to myself then. These are the things

I used to remind myself daily. Gender neutral.
Only use gender neutral when you must talk
about your beloved. And never speak of love.

It will only invite questions. So much to learn.
Memorize all of it. Know it well enough to recite
it backwards if you must. Every last detail.

The expected heart rate of a newborn? The exact
percentage of fats, protein, and carbohydrates
in Total Parenteral Nutrition? The formulae

for calculating blood volume? Everything.
You have no time for the personal.
And that morning, on my last day in the NICU?

Do I remember it? I do. I still remember it.
And this is what I say to myself now: You must
remember it. Along with the calculations, the hours

and hours of sick babies, you must remember it.
That woman, your teacher, grilled you for 35 minutes,
question after question after question. She did it

in plain sight, in front of all the nurses, the residents,
the interns, the clerks, the other students. She wanted
you to answer incorrectly, wanted to shame you.

Question after question after question, you hid
behind correct facts and information. And when
she tired of the game, of trying to trip you up,

she announced for everyone that you were the best
minority student she had ever had. And you took it.
You wanted to be like a duck, to let it all wash off of you.

But even in that praise, there was venom. Even in praise,
she found a way to shame you, single you out. And you hid
behind correct answers. But now, you must make it personal.

Sepsis

The fog has yet to lift, God, and still the bustle
of buses and garbage trucks. God, I have coveted
sleep. I have wished to find an empty bed

in the hospital while on call. I have placed
my bodily needs first, left nurses to do
what I should have done. And so, the antibiotics

sat on the counter. They sat on the counter
under incandescent lights. No needle was placed
in the woman's arm. No IV was started. It sat there

on the counter waiting. I have coveted sleep, God,
and the toxins I studied in Bacteriology took hold
of Your servant. When the blood flowered

beneath her skin, I shocked her, placed the paddles
on her chest, her dying body convulsing each time.
The antibiotics sat on the counter, and shame

colored my face, the blood pooling in my cheeks
like heat. And outside, the stars continued falling
into place. And the owl kept talking without listening.

And the wind kept sweeping the streets clean.
And the heart in my chest stayed silent.
How could I have known that I would never forget,

that early some mornings, in the waking time,
the fog still filling the avenues, that the image
of her body clothed in sweat would find me?

I have disobeyed my Oath. I have caused harm.
I have failed the preacher from the Baptist Church.
Dear God, how does a sinner outlast the sin?

Against Divination

The smudge pots' smoke foretold more than the frost
we expected. Somewhere, in the center of the grove,
the men huddled together to examine the beautiful

yellow-green rot consuming the wayward branch
of the orange tree lying on the ground, examined
the break in the wood to divine something about

the nature of the situation. What surprises is their need
to know and predict peril. The drama of peril.
The pulse quickening, the blood pressure rising

until we feel the vibration in our knees. Divination:
by smoke, by fire, by mirror, by water itself. I have
forgotten which one truly predicts the certainty of peril.

And because you have opened up another, because you have
examined the cells of another, seen for yourself that we are
primarily water, do you, too, have that ancient power?

Today, the tears from the woman who tells me her doctor
gave her *six months*. Oh the gift of scrying, the gift of prophecy.
There are twelve types of rot for the orange tree,

but for the sake of mystery, I do not name them.
And for the way demise inches down the leaves
of the tiger lily, there are two names, verbs even.

That water holds the past, present, and the future
is nothing new. Hippocrates, having examined tears,
suspected as much. Over the years, I have perfected

my suturing, have studied the tension of suture between
my hand and the resisting tissue, learned how it reveals
whether the closure will hold. The smudge pots' smoke

foretold more than we could ever have expected—
there would be frost and the threat of frost, fire
and the fire of rot racing throughout the grove.

My attempts to depict that scene were failures. Once,
I even tried to paint three doctors: one with his ears
sewn shut, another, his eyes. Likewise, I never finished

that painting, never completed the final doctor whose eyes
are dark, menacing, and wide. Someday, I will close his mouth
with red suture; I will conjure silence for that terrible oracle.

Deus ex machina

Even the intangible can be broken.
Maybe it would be better for me to say
that things just go wrong, or that things

aren't always harmonious. At the start
of Saint-Saëns' *Danse Macabre*, a tritone,
an augmented Fourth, stands in for the Devil.

The violin itself must be tuned especially for this.
You think I am lying, but I am not lying.
Not the Ghost in the machine, but the Devil

in the instrument. Things go wrong. Things
sometimes go terribly wrong. And some of us
are attracted to this. We want to fix things.

As children, we were the ones who fixed anything—
mechanical, electronic, any malfunctioning machine
could be fixed, our tool-like fingers responding

to a fidgety, overactive imagination. Is that not
what calls some of us to the "healing arts,"
that strange desire to fix the human machine?

But all things broken cannot be fixed; the man,
whose eyes never meet my own, tells me
his spirit is broken, his spirit is crushed

(his words, not mine). And what can I
say to that? What tools do I have to fix that?
Not these hands, not this brain

looking for other instruments besides these hands,
not this voice that is trying now to reassure him:
It will be okay... Believe me, things will be fine...

Nothing is working. He tells me this. Nothing
is working. And tomorrow, the nurse will offer me
a scrap of newspaper, will silently enter my office

and say nothing. When I read about how
he hanged himself in his garage, no amount
of tears or wringing of hands will fix it.

Torn

There was the knife and the broken syringe
then the needle in my hand, the Tru-Cut
followed by the night-blue suture.

The wall behind registration listed a man
with his face open. Through the glass doors,
I saw the sky going blue to black as it had

24 hours earlier when I last stood there gazing off
into space, into the nothingness of that town.
Bat to the head. Knife to the face. They tore

down the boy in an alleyway, the broken syringe
skittering across the sidewalk. No concussion.
But the face torn open, the blood congealed

and crusted along his cheek. *Stitch up the faggot
in bed 6* is all the ER doctor had said.
Queasy from the lack of sleep, I steadied

my hands as best as I could after cleaning up
the dried blood. There was the needle
and the night-blue suture trailing behind it.

There was the flesh torn and the skin open.
I sat there and threw stitch after stitch
trying to put him back together again.

When the tears ran down his face,
I prayed it was a result of my work
and not the work of the men in the alley.

Even though I knew there were others to be seen,
I sat there and slowly threw each stitch.
There were always others to be seen. There was

always the bat and the knife. I said nothing,
and the tears kept welling in his eyes.
And even though I was told to be "quick and dirty,"

told to spend less than 20 minutes, I sat there
for over an hour closing the wound so that each edge
met its opposing match. I wanted him

to be beautiful again. *Stitch up the faggot in bed 6.*
Each suture thrown reminded me I would never be safe
in that town. There would always be the bat

and the knife, always a fool willing to tear me open
to see the dirty faggot inside. And when they
came in drunk or high with their own wounds,

when they bragged about their scuffles with the knife
and that other world of men, I sat there and sutured.
I sat there like an old woman and sewed them up.

Stitch after stitch, the slender exactness of my fingers
attempted perfection. I sat there and sewed them up.

from *The Halo* (2016)

Eclipse

Admit it. You return to your past because you
have gained some kind of knowledge to interpret it:
the titanium device with its four pins meticulously
buried in your skull, sunlight from the window
reflecting off its edges to cast fractured lines of light

across your chest and across your hospital bed,
these rays of light appearing to beam from this metal ring
around your head (like a goddamned angel), or
how when your nurse flicks it with his plastic pen
it vibrates in a key you cannot yet name. Call it

the key of metal, of titanium, of shiny misfortune.
Admit it, the present is awfully dull and will remain so
until many years later when it comes miraculously
into focus, when you understand all four meanings
of the word *regret*. So it is you go back, armed now

with this word *halo*, word rife with what
you have learned about how angels were depicted
in Renaissance painting, the ring or rings of light painted
by the old masters so as to hover lightly around the head.
And how can you not see with this knowledge, knowing

as you do now about those terrible wings you keep
and continue to keep secret? Some would argue
we keep secrets because we cannot help ourselves.
But what if secrets are kept simply because we have yet
to make sense of what really happened?

The moon in latest afternoon, just days ago, hid
a segment of the setting sun, and there before us a *mandorla*
without even a faint sketch of a god or angel beneath it.
Admit it, I am not alone: things beg for significance.
Would that we always had time to come back to them…

Annunciation

I learned to hide my wings almost immediately,
learned to tuck and bandage them down.
Long before the accident, before the glass shattering
and that scene going dim, dimmer, and then dark,
before the three fractures at the axis, three cracks

in the bone, it had already begun. My voice
had begun to deepen, the sound of it
suddenly more my father's than my own. My beard
had started growing, my bones growing, my bones
sore from the speed of their growth, and there,

at fourteen years of age, the first tugging
of the muscles between my shoulder blades.
It began as a tiny ache. It was just a minor irritation.
Day after day passed, and this ache grew,
and then the tips of the cartilaginous wings

began to tent my skin. Father Callahan
had already warned that in each of us
there was both potential for bad and good.
When trying to shave for the first time, I nicked
my cheek, the bleeding slow but continuous.

Standing there, dabbing at this small cut with tissue paper,
the first tear surprised me, the left wing heaving through
that fleshy mound of muscle between my shoulder blades
and then the skin. I buckled and, on my knees, the right wing
presented itself more rapidly than the left.

When I stood, there in the mirror, my wings outstretched
with their tiny feathers wet, almost glutinous, a quick
ribbon of blood snaking down my back. You wonder
why I am such a master of avoidance, such a master
of what is withheld. Is there any wonder, now?

The Gods Among Us

One of them grants you the ability
to forecast the future; another wrenches
your tongue from your mouth, changes you
into a bird precisely because you have been
given this gift. The gods are generous

in this way. I learned to avoid danger, avoid fear,
avoid excitement, these the very triggers that prompt
my wings from their resting place deep inside.
And so, I avoided fights, avoided everything really.
In the locker room, I avoided other boys,

all the while intently studying that space
between their shoulder blades, patiently looking
for the tell-tale signs, looking to find even
one other boy like me, the wings buried but
there nonetheless. I studied them from a distance.

When people challenge a god, the gods curse them
with the label of madness. It is all very convenient.
And meanwhile, a god took the form of a swan
and raped a girl by the school gates. Another
took the shape of an eagle to abduct a boy

from the football field. Mad world.
And what about our teachers? Our teachers
expected us to sit and listen. In Theology, there was
a demon inside each of us; in History,
the demons among us. So many demons

in this world. Who among us could have spoken up
against the gods, the gods who continued living
among us? They granted wishes and punishments
much the way they always had. Very few noticed them
casually taking the shape of one thing or another.

The Hanged Man

I know a lot about the second cervical vertebra.
And because I love precision and accuracy, I refer
to it as the axis, its name buried in Latin,
meaning *chariot*, meaning *axle*, meaning the line
around which something revolves or turns.

How is that for being exact? And to break the axis,
to fracture it, is rare. A neurosurgeon will tell you
it comprises only 15% of cervical spine injuries.
Although we live in the 21st century and one
would assume a more clinical name for breaking

the axis, such a break is still called the Hangman's
Fracture. I need not explain the derivation
of such a name. Not divers or thrill-seekers,
but heretics and those charged with treason
provided such a term—the hanged man, the monster,

the witch and the unloved. Go ahead; break this bone.
Shatter it. Leave cracks to be seen on an x-ray.
The hanged man walking tilts his head to the side
opposite the cracks. He tilts his head away from
such an insult. He tries to appear normal.

But there is no name for such behavior,
no clinical name to describe this odd activity of avoidance.
I have spent years studying avoidance. I am
an expert now. I never say the hip bone is connected
to the thigh bone. I say acetabulum, say head of the femur.

An Ordinary Boy

A fascicle of feathers in my hand, hand
frantic and shaking, my arm holding my hand
as far away from my body as possible—I am disgusted.
I cannot pull out the central stalks of my wings
where they protrude from between my shoulder blades,

but I can strip every tuft of feathers from them
to bare those cartilaginous stems as they rise
from my back, stalks stripped perfectly
clean so as to better tuck them along my spine,
hide them, make them invisible beneath my clothing.

I was so foolish then, a teenager not yet able
to accept what he was. When my wings blackened,
withered, and fell off, I was beyond happy.
They would stay dormant sometimes as long as
three months. Sadly, they always came back.

In the bathroom mirror, I can see myself offering
a cluster of feathers to myself, as if to say:
Take this from me and I will be forever grateful.
But the me that is a trick of light on glass
is uncaring, offers them back immediately.

If I concentrate, if I think hard on it, I can move
my wings, and I practice in the bathroom mirror.
But these wings cannot support my weight,
cannot buoy me on even a strong gust of wind.
What good are wings if you cannot fly?

What good is this ridiculous secret I am asked
to keep? With the feathers ripped cleanly away,
I tuck the stems along my spine. I bandage them down—
cloth wound under my armpits, tightly wound
around my chest. I fashion myself into an ordinary boy.

Mind Over Matter

Things repeat themselves—mirror themselves—
sometimes with only a slight variation, the edges
of a bloom, perhaps, tinged in rust instead of alizarin.
But the bloom remains the same. Just so, the lily
repeats itself each spring, surprising even the shrubbery

in Golden Gate Park with its shock of white, at times
milk white. I have photographs to prove this, photographs
in which these blooms each year appear in almost the same place.
It is like magic, dark magic. No one can explain it to me.
Which theorem helps us understand how these blooms

arrive again and again in similar and predictable spaces?
Once upon a time, I watched motion-capture photography
bring a flower's previous bloom back to sit in view
of its current incarnation. Ah, the miracle of optics
and the science of a dark room. Once upon a time,

I woke to find myself cradled in a bed, the hospital room
streaked with light and shadow from half-opened blinds.
I tried to move but could not. I saw the metallic light
reflected from the halo around my head. I saw a doctor
standing by my bedside studying me, his furrowed brow

tempered by a half-smile. As my eyes grew accustomed to the light, this doctor faded away. The brain can lie, but this was no trick. The man standing over me was me. This man had come to assure me I would live, that I would become the very man I did not want to become.

Bloodline

In that old story, the boy is depicted as delicate,
lithe, and beautiful. Ovid had it wrong.
Yes, the boy was beautiful, beautiful enough
to capture a god's attention, but he was not
delicate. He was anything but delicate,

his muscles toned from working the fields.
Listen to me; the gods are fairly conventional.
A lovely woman is transformed into
an old hag, a too-slow voyeur becomes
the quick stag to be chased and shot through

by a single arrow. So, in the case of this young man,
he must have been strong, anything but delicate
like these flowers. The gods are convincing
when they need to be. Believe me, they are
honey-mouthed and persistent. The boy

had to be strong, but he was not stronger than the gods.
He was seduced; who isn't seduced by
immortality? In the field, the boy was every bit
the archer as the god. He was just as powerful
with a spear, a slingshot, or a discus.

Ovid writes that Apollo loved the boy,
loved him more than any living thing
on this earth. But we know better.
The gods love only themselves. In the field,
a clearing ringed by trees, the boy did not

try to catch the discus. He was running from it,
running from the god who took pains to aim
so as to slice him clean through with a single shot.
You see, this is not love. A god commanding
spilled blood become delicate blue flowers is not love.

After Crossing the *Via Appia*

One must never trust in hearing. One should trust,
instead, in the smell of burning rubber,
the sight of glass shattering and then rushing away
from your very skin, skin vibrating the way it does
before sex or after a light rain. Because…. Because.

Because my wings had already erupted from between
my shoulder blades. Because I had coveted
another man in that secret space in my own head,
the lean shape of him, his water-drenched skin as he rose
from the sea off Fort Lauderdale Beach. Because I

had been weak, had questioned Father Callahan
about the body of Christ. One should not covet.
Thou shalt not covet. And who was I to question
the workings of the divine? Thou shalt not question
things that are holy and beyond question.

Because Aquinas, too, had been on the Appian Way.
Because he, too, had hit his head and would never
be loved by the divine. Because he could not
be trusted, because he knew too well the teachings
of Aristotle. Because he lied in that way we all lie.

In that bed in which I lay motionless, my mind could not
comprehend the fire felt but not visible. Even now,
one wants to interrogate, to call on the wide sky above
and ask it *why*. The simple mind never learns its lesson.
It never learns. It never learns. It never learns.

Ruins

The sand dotted with trash and detritus,
and out over the horizon that first hint of light
betrayed sunrise was coming, the Atlantic
not as wine dark as it had been an hour earlier.
One walks among ruins to remind oneself

that progress is made at any cost. You
had come to the beach late the night before
because a man had promised you
he could walk on water, had promised
to show you this, you doubting Thomas.

You believed his gin-soaked detailing,
believed he could slowly and carefully float out
over water, and you thought he was like you.
But all he did was walk on the sand, earth-bound
and unbalanced. He had neither wings

nor the ability to fly. And when he removed
your shirt and felt the stumps between your
shoulder blades, your wings dormant, buried beneath
your flesh, he wanted to show you every ability he had
except that of flight. People lie. Lessons like these

are always difficult. A reckless sun tilted at the edge
of the horizon, and then the gulls arrived to begin
their studies, their lonely scavenging.
And my small lesson? Human to want the company
of others, and human, too, to find loneliness among them.

In Pursuit

Her feet, at first racing through the trees
with the quickness of an antelope, her body
throwing itself forward, hurling itself, the speed
of it like a drug, the speed of it
a necessary thing to escape the god

—no one has yet to convince me her father's response
to her cries for help was a blessing—then her feet
slowing and denser, growing heavy, heavy,
then fixed, her toes curling into the dirt
and taking root, the bark rising up

from the surface of her skin, her skin
prickling and tender as the bark restrained her,
her arms suddenly captured in the motion of surrender,
her arms held out on either side of her,
her hair falling out and then leaves,

newly green, almost silver, ripping through
her skin, through the bark, the leaves delicate and fine,
leaves marking her not as a young woman but as
a tree, a laurel tree, the very leaves torn from her and
fashioned into a crown by the god.

So few of these transformations are ever a blessing.
So, it isn't as if I had been lacking preparation.
You could say I had studied for it, sat patiently
with those old metamorphoses for years. My
shy hunter has never read these tales, would

likely find them silly. What he says is *See that grouse
over there? Shoot it.* And I do. I don't even
question it. Sometimes, my skin feels prickly,
and I wonder if another transformation is about
to take place. But no one is ever transformed twice.

No one. Ovid understood this. Even Suetonius
understood this. The gods have little use for us once
we have been changed. They take the laurel leaves,
scorn the wounded bird, erase their tell-tale foot prints,
busy themselves with the generous work of gods.

The Vista

Not tenderness in the eye but a brute need
to see accurately: over the ridge on a trail
deep in Tennessee, the great poet looked out
and examined the vista that confederate soldiers saw
as they rode over its edge rather than surrender.

I saw only the cliff's edge and then
estimated the distance down to the bottom
of that dirty ravine. This is what someone with wings
does when he knows he cannot fly: he measures
distance. I have spent far too much time

examining my wings in the bathroom mirror
after the shower's steam has evaporated
from the medicine cabinet's toothpaste-spattered glass:
grey, each feather just slightly bigger than a hawk's.
The great poet said one might find a vista like this,

perhaps, once in a lifetime, but I didn't understand
what he meant by this then. My wings, tucked
beneath my t-shirt, beneath my long-sleeved oxford,
my wings folded in along my spine, were irritated
by that humid air, itchy from collecting sweat after hiking.

I wasn't paying attention, which is a sin I have since learned.
At 14, after the wings first erupted from my back,
I went up to the roof and tried to fly. Some lessons
can only be learned after earnest but beautiful failures.
My individual feathers are just slightly bigger than a hawk's

feathers. My wingspan is just about 8 feet. I'm a man,
and like men I measure everything. But vistas
make me nervous. And the great poet made me nervous.
And I knew then what I still know now, that I
was only seconds away from another beautiful failure.

Praise

The hawk need not measure distance.
It need not estimate its time from drift or glide
to the lightning bolt necessary to pluck
a chick from the edge of the yard.
Apollo's messenger, his cleanest predator—its beak

is perfect, its talons perfect, its hunger and its
manipulation of air perfect. You have to respect
the hawk. Over the field, I watch one circle and circle
tracing the symbol for infinity. Even at this
distance, I can see the rustling grass

that betrays not wind but an animal.
From the movement of the long grass, I
predict rodent, field rat. And when the infinite,
those connecting circles of sway and glide
become lightning, become strike, it happens

in mere seconds. One spies the rodent's shape
clutched in the talons of that incredible machine.
We all have talents, gifts some call them.
Some of us live out our entire lives
blissfully unaware of these so-called gifts.

I can measure distance. I can estimate
distance from thing to another,
from hawk to the *terra firma* of the field,
from one person to another. This is what
someone with wings does when he knows

he cannot fly. I respect the hawk. It
is a machine, Apollo's cleanest predator, his
gentle reminder. When my shy hunter stands
at the edge of the field, I scan the distance between us.
I wish to be silent in this air. I wish to be lightning.

The Sixth Sense

I am reminded a dove is often heard before
it is seen, reminded that a rifle is an extension of
the man. I am reminded of so much this morning,
the rifle's weight awkward in my hands.
Lock the target, sense the line, let the gun

do its job. Must everything in life
sound so mystical? Out in the field
two wild turkeys mope and saunter;
they know we are after birds of the air and not
those that prefer the field. I am reminded that

we are also creatures that prefer fields.
Trust your hearing, I am told. But my hearing
isn't my best sense. And that keen sense of sight
I inherited seems strangely limited on the ground,
in this clearing where the field is ringed

by a rampart of trees. Lock the target. I have
no target. Trust your hearing, he repeats.
And when I say hawk before its shadow
crosses over our heads, before sound or sight
can confirm it, I am labeled prey

instead of hunter. The joke is that only a bird
senses the presence of a stronger bird.
You are prey, he laughs. *You're a strange bird.*
When I turn quickly and fire my rifle over his head,
a distant dove suddenly forced to contend with gravity,

my shy hunter is as pale as an apparition. A rifle is
an extension of the man, I respond. Somewhere
in the distance, the hawk wheels and disappears
into a stand of trees. Despite everything, he is right,
my shy hunter. I know this. I know I am prey.

Human Wishes

In order to prove to a hunter you are not
prey, you have to kill him. It's that simple.
There are no *ifs ands* or *buts* about it.
My shy hunter was a model for me, a model
of a man. But I am not a man.

An accident, some kind of hybrid, I am a monster.
I thank the generous god who prompted wings
from inside my back, thank the god who
gave me the keenness of sight, my ability
to harness all of my senses, gave me speed.

I thank the drunk woman who ran a red light,
the result being deep sleep, thank her for
crippling me, for leaving three cracks in the bone
to be seen on an x-ray. I thank the many failures
that came of these events, because I am a grateful

thing. I am grateful. I wanted most of all to be a man,
an ordinary man. I suppose that is the most human
aspect of me, the want. Real men hunt. So, what choice
did I have but to apprentice myself to this hunter?
My shy hunter says *Tell me what you see in the field.*

And I do. I catalog hiding places. I list off
potential targets without batting an eye.
When I list him as one of the things I see,
his only response is to chuckle and remind me
he is a person and not a thing, not an animal.

There are no *ifs ands* or *buts* about it.
You already know what happens. You already know
how this story ends. How could you not? I removed
my shirt, the bandages, too. My wings unfurled.
And when I raised the rifle and told him to run, he ran.

The Halo

In the paintings left to us
by the Old Masters, the halo,
a smallish cloud of light, clung
to the head, carefully framed the faces
of mere mortals made divine.

Accident? My body launched
by a car's incalculable momentum?
It ended up outside the car. I had no idea then
what it was like to lose days, to wake
and find everything had changed.

Through glass, this body went
through the glass window, the seatbelt
snapping my neck. Not the hanged man,
not a man made divine but more human.
I remember those pins buried in my skull,

the cold metal frame surrounding my head,
metal reflecting a small fire, a glow. All
was changed. In that bed, I was a locust.
I was starving. And how could I not be?
I, I, I... I am still ravenous.

from *Prometeo* (2021)

For Its Blue Flickering

If you take cobalt as a simple salt
and dissolve it—if you dip a small metal loop
in such a solution and place it in a standard

flame, it burns a brilliant blue,
the flame itself bluer than the richest of skies
in summer. I wanted to be that blue.

And so, I claimed that element as my own,
imagined that fire could make of me
something bluer than the bluest of blues.

But what does an eighteen-year-old boy know
of the blues? All I knew then of cobalt
was its stable isotope. I had no knowledge

of the radioactive one with its gamma rays
used for decades to treat cancer. I had yet
to be exposed to such a thing. I was hot

for cobalt, for its blue flickering. Chemistry
can be such an odd thing. When a teacher of mine
offered up that faggots doused in certain chemicals

burned blue, I saw it as a sign; how can we
not see such things as signs, as omens?
Blue the waters of the Caribbean Sea,

blue the skies over the high deserts,
and "blue" the passages I found in old Greek texts
that surprised my prudish sense

of what men could do with men. It always
came back to blue. But boyish ideas are just that.
They seem for all the world to be fixed things,

when all they are is merely fleeting. In the end,
my make up was none other than anthracite,
something cold, dark, and difficult to ignite.

It is dense, only semi-lustrous, and hardly
noticeable. One dreams in cobalt, but one lives
in anthracite. Yes, the analogy is that basic.

Anthracite, one of earth's studies in difficulty:
once lit it burns and burns. Caught somewhere
between ordinary coal and extraordinary graphite,

anthracite surprises when it burns. It isn't flashy—
it produces a short, blue, and smokeless flame
that reminds one of the heart more than the sky.

At Lake Merced

Some men go down to the river.
I went down, instead, to the lake: the air
silent and stretched tightly over it,

the water unmoved and dangerously still.
Some men move past such a scene
without even the slightest notice of it.

But this morning, a man in a shell
rowed across this lake's smoothed surface,
the tip of his shell leaving a widening V

behind it, the shell cleanly slicing through
the water like an arrow, the way an arrow slices
through air or flesh. And just like that, the image

of the Saint pierced through by arrows becomes
fixed within my head, the arrows all leaving V's
behind them, V for violence, as if the very air

were an impasto on canvas. And just like that,
the arrows slicing through the air become bullets,
each one leaving its V behind it, the paint

at the target dabbed with a red duller than crimson.
You may wonder why on earth a man shot through
centuries ago would appear to me upon seeing this

tiny shell of a boat crossing a lake, but the present day
does a remarkable job of emulating the past. Let us
leave it at that. Some men find nothing, and others

find omens everywhere. The stillness of the air
above the lake; the shell slicing through the water;
the Saint shot through with arrows yet living, breathing,

his chest heaving, his head slumping while the arms remain
perfectly still, and the brown boy shot through
with bullets, his wounds a red duller than crimson:

things like this still happen almost every day.

Mestizaje

At the ruins of Tulum, on a boulder
half-buried in sand on the famous beach
below the often-photographed pyramid
that stares out at the sea, I found

a petroglyph overlaid in white chalk
to better demonstrate the bird-like thing
carved into its side. I had seen it before.
In Cuba, maybe, or Puerto Rico, somewhere

on one of the islands out across this sea
watched over here by trees and pyramids.
The bird, on this boulder, like the one
I had seen elsewhere, had only one leg.

But this should come as no surprise, the Taíno
having left this soil many hundreds of years ago
to search for new land, new coastlines.
They made landfall all across the Antilles

and flourished there until the Spaniards arrived.
As the textbooks will tell you, the Taíno are
extinct, the people and their culture
extinguished by Spain long ago. But tell that

to the old brujas, the old island women
who will proclaim we are of this dirt
and can send any man who stands against us
back to the dirt. The irony of this is legion.

One did not need a laboratory to cross
the tangerine with the grapefruit to make
the tangelo, and the Spaniards did not need
a laboratory to cross the Taíno with themselves.

So, when I stand here on this beach at Tulum,
is it any wonder we all look like cousins?
Not the Spaniards who dabbled in the witchcraft
of mestizaje, not the Spaniards who claimed

all of this region as their own—no, it is
the Taíno, cousins to the Maya, that link us.
Peer into the DNA of many Caribbean people,
and you will find that 10-20% of it

is indigenous, is Taíno. We are of this dirt. We cannot
be killed off, the old women say. And in the base pairs
of our DNA, we discover the truth. One can hide
many things, but the truth is always there.

An ancient god buried himself in the dirt that gave
rise to the Taíno. And with time, the Taíno themselves
were buried. This is all true. But they are not dead.
No, no, not dead. They are buried within us.

The Point

His other doctors proclaimed that he would die
     within a month. He kept on living for years:
the simple fact is that he was barely thirty

     but had been dying for almost two of them.
The urge for prophecy is deep and deeply
     rooted inside the gnarled and human heart—

we seek it out, its shiny metallic edge.
     The cancer spread to his bones and then his liver.
Each time it reappeared, we treated it

     with radiation; we stalled it, held it back,
until it spread to his lungs making every treatment
     that I proposed seem less and less an option.

So this is it? You're just going to let me die?
     Mano, you leave me here to die like this?
But here, you see, the tongue is wiser than

     a knife, the word selected not just "brother" but
a word that cut far deeper than English ever could.
     The urge to prophecy is deep but not a given.

I gave no answer. I gave him nothing more.
      And when I tried to rest my hand against
his arm, he turned away from me and said

      to leave him, leave him now, to which he added
Mano, again, to drive the sharpened point home.
      The fact is he was barely thirty years old,

and I had failed him, run out of things to try.
      Not even I could blame him for that finely-
honed stab, that carefully-chosen Spanish word.

      To some, the owl is a symbol of death to come.
For others, it is the guardian that ferries souls.
      I'm still not sure to which one I subscribe.

But there was not an owl in sight that morning,
      barely a week since trying to talk to him,
and nothing to see outside except the dark.

      I knew that something was off, was terribly wrong,
no matter how I tried to calm my mind.
      I stood there thinking, thinking about it all:

our final conversation, my failures, what now?
      I tried to reassure myself that I
had done all that I could have done for him.

      Some of us study the future, and others the past.
It makes no difference at all. At work that day,
      his sister called to let me know he died.

He passed that morning just before the sun
      had started rising. Why I knew this then,
knew it before the news had yet to come,

      troubles me even to this day. Not English,
not "brother," bother buried within the word.
      Instead, the Spanish word he knew would leave

a mark, would slice to the bone, sharp as a knife.

Portrait in Salt and Dusky Carmine

As in childhood, the gentility of verandas
and gardens, of tea and its trappings, made me
anxious. But it took very little time for one
to disappear from that world. The cane fields

that separate civility from the rough shoreline
allow anyone, upper crust or field hand, to disappear.
Down one of many dirt rows, the line cut as straight
as the cane planted on either side, one rushes

from the cultured world to an untouched one.
Out of the cane fields, out from its wind-rippled leaves
shepherding you onward, one finds the sand
and sea awaiting as if discarded by a retired god.

The setting sun's red and orange fingers tried,
unsuccessfully, to reconfigure the seven shades
the water's varying depths reflected, but all
that changed was the sea foam once white now pink.

The English painter, who visited here once, wrote
that the daily gaudiness of this sight made one
long for the nuance of dimming light at dusk
as it smudged its charcoal over a Hampshire field.

All I can say is it takes a certain temperament
to prefer a sunset in Hampshire to a sunset
in the Caribbean. I do not have such a temperament.
I prefer a scene that requires oils instead of charcoal.

The shore empty, the sun no longer visible,
the water's colors finally succumbed and darkened
to night, the same as that settling over us from above.
Not the sunset, but the time following sunset:

the day's Technicolor displays erased. Alone
on the soft sand, the surf mumbled the old language.
Like my great grandmother who visits me
in dreams, it said: *Salt or no salt, trust no one.*

It is difficult for one like me to disregard the sea
and the cane fields. I am perfectly aware this place
is no longer my home, but the sea says *Truth is truth*,
and the cane field says *Like the machete, you belong to me.*

The Call

in memoriam Cecil Young

I am addicted to words, constantly ferret them away
in anticipation. You cannot accuse me of not being prepared.
I am ready for anything. I can create an image faster than

just about anyone. And so, the crows blurring the tree line;
the sky's light dimming and shifting; the Pacific cold and
impatient as ever: this is just the way I feel. Nothing more.

I could gussy up those crows, transform them
into something more formal, more Latinate, could use
the exact genus *Corvus*, but I won't. Not today.

Like any addict, I, too, have limits. And I have written
too many elegies already. The Living have become
jealous of the amount I have written for the Dead.

So, leave the crows perched along the tree line
watching over us. Leave them be. The setting sun?
Leave it be. For God's sake, what could be easier

in a poem about death than a setting sun? Leave it be.
Words cannot always help you, the old poet had taught
me, cannot always be there for you no matter how you

store them away with sharpened forethought.
Not the courier in his leather sandals, his legs dark and dirty
from the long race across the desert. Not the carrier

pigeon arriving with the news of another dead Caesar
and the request you present yourself. Nothing like that.
The telephone rings. Early one morning, the telephone rings

and the voice is your mother's voice. No fanfare. Your
father's brother is dead. He died that morning. And your tongue
went silent. Like any other minor poet, you could not find

the best words, the appropriate words. Leave it be now.
You let your mother talk and talk to fill the silence. Leave it be.
All of your practiced precision, all of the words saved up

for a poem, can do nothing to remedy that now.

Portrait in Sugar and Simple Prayer

The language of sugar isn't difficult
to master. One learns it as easily as

any other tongue. You may not believe me,
but it is true. As a boy, lost in the cane fields,

I made a mistake (Who doesn't make mistakes?)
and, for this small error, I was punished, the sweet

sugar cane becoming weapon, becoming punisher.
Each time the man brought the body

of the cane stalk down across my back,
I cried out. Would you believe me if I told you

that today I wouldn't even whimper at such a thing?
Because now I know how to brandish a stalk,

how to bring it down as testament, how to make
the nothing of air sing before the strike. And because,

well, now I know how to accept punishment as well.
You punish or are punished. It really is that simple.

Dominus, Holy Father, I have hidden myself
in the cane field. I may have sinned. My back is bare

and in need of your administrations. Not salt
in the wound, Lord, but sugar. Sugar as sharp

as the metallic taste of blood in the mouth.
Make me regret this, Lord. Make me...

Strike me, Lord, strike me harder than any man.
Make of me something sweeter than sugar.

Precatio simplex

in memoriam Mavis Clarke

Father, Holy Father, Prime Mover, God Almighty—
I have forgotten what to call you. Standing here
before the Pacific, I am tempted to call you

Poseidon, Green Neptune, someone I understand
more clearly than I have ever understood You.
The sea's slow tide, its almost-hidden riptide dragging

handfuls of foam under the surface, has no answers
for me. Sitting here on the crest of the sand dunes,
there is no one by my side. I have come here

alone because I remember what the nuns
taught me, that You do not appreciate a show
of these things. Not success with words, not

the lottery prize now worth millions, not the
usual things I am sure others request: I come now
to ask for something unthinkable for one like me.

Almost 3,000 miles away, near the brighter coast
of this godless country, my aunt's pain is
outpacing the cancer tearing her abdomen apart.

No amount of morphine can break it. I do not
come to ask You for miracles. I know better
than to ask for miracles. I know the world

is filled with miracles. No, no, not miracles.
Take her right now, Father. Here stands the cancer doctor
asking you to take his aunt because he cannot stomach

the idea of her in so much pain. Send me a small sign:
wheeling gulls, a sudden gust of wind, anything. Anything.
Just this once, Holy Father, don't let me down.

Cancer

in memoriam Paul Otremba

One must be trained to locate it. One finds it
by finding the Lion first and then the Brothers.
The faintest of the 13 signs in the night sky,

we have learned to see it by discerning what flanks it.
You were right that evening in Vermont to say
it doesn't even look like a crab. I joked it looked

more like an upside-down Y, more like the Greek
λ, a symbol which, for me, had more to do with
radioactivity calculations used in radiation therapy.

I was showing off, you see, making sure I would be seen
as a doctor as well as a writer. But by then we were
already close enough for you to forgive my arrogance.

But your question came quickly: *How do you do it
every day? All those people with cancer...* We stared
at the stars, and I recounted a sordid story

about an old poet we admired. The stars,
the resulting story, and your laughter: the things
memory made indelible. You knew it was the veins

spreading out in a solid tumor seen when cut and examined
that reminded Hippocrates of the crab, something
far less poetic than the stars seen in the night sky,

but that is how you chose to think about it. And because
oncologists always think of cancer, I purposely chose
to think of reflux when, over lunch two years ago, you

kept coughing, kept choking. Later, you told me
that as you lay in the scanner you loved the idea of light
passing through you, photons used to look inside your chest.

Even then, you chose the poetic. Your greatest fear
was that the biopsy might discover an ulcer leading to
restrictions on fine food and wine. Instead, they found the crab.

.

You were born under the sign of the scorpion, but I
always saw you as a Lion. A brother, I assumed you were safely
distanced from the crab. Let the light pass through you now.

Not the photons we manipulate for Medicine,
but the starlight that has traveled with us for millennia.
We need not look for the Lion or the Brothers anymore.

Portrait in Ochre and Seven Whispers

i.

To make and remake one's self is
the artist's job, I believed. And so, in poems,
I gave myself wings. But even then, I made sure
the wings could not support flight, could not
lift me to safety. Even my imagination failed me.

ii.

The first time I tried to kill myself, I swallowed
a bottle of Tylenol, pill after pill, like the sacrament
of communion, placed on my tongue.

iii.

You were supposed to save us. You were
supposed to help save our souls. Isn't that part
of the vow you made to God when choosing
the life you did? You must have forgotten that.
You didn't kill my soul. But you didn't save it either.

iv.

I'm never late anymore, never late to anything.
Because I still wonder if I hadn't dawdled after practice,
if I had showered with the other boys instead of
waiting, if… There are always so many *ifs*.
Would you have stopped if I had screamed, if I had
fought harder? I still find it so easy to list off the *ifs*.

v.

My second lie came when I woke, in the hospital,
and told my parents I swallowed the pills
because I was being bullied at school.
An easy lie. Much easier than the truth. The third lie?
The promise I would never try to kill myself again.

vi.

The woman killing my parents, the sudden
and uncontrolled rising from the ground as people

gawked and screamed, the vomiting up of gold coins:
dreams I have had repeatedly over all these years.

vii.

I found your obituary, the memorial, the pictures
of you as a kindly old priest. You are dead now.
I wanted to write my own statement for you,
to shame you, to tell the world how you pinned
the 13-year-old me to the wall in a gym's shower,
put your hands around my neck, and sodomized me.
But shame is never an equal transaction, is it? Shame,
the one thing I cannot live with, cannot live without.

Portrait in Graphite and Ornamental Hagiography

You may not believe it, but I have tried,
set my sights on the morning star
in belief it would guide me. I have tried.

I have tried, as the Jesuits taught, to be
singular, to be whole, to be one. The labor
of this was exhausting. Time reveals things

one need not appreciate when young, and I fear
being singular, being one, is something
damned near impossible for someone

like me. Saint Jerome, cloistered in a tiny room,
found his singular calling in updating
the Latin Bible with his knowledge of Greek texts.

In Assisi, Saint Francis updated nature, called birds
out of the trees. I am, unfortunately, no saint.
Fractured, divided to the quick, I am incapable

of being singular. And the old nun who taught Art
at my high school, who called me a stupid mongrel,
understood this very fact long before I did.

Profession, family, belief: I can see now
my background challenges me, prevents me
from remaining true to only one thing. The fog,

settled over Ocean Beach, settles the matter
by embracing everything indiscriminately,
and I want to understand why I notice

such things. For most of my life, I have desired
a category, a designation, but maybe
that desire was misplaced? Maybe it was just

another failure, a failure of imagination?
Outside, two hummingbirds cross-stitch the air.
They have lived here for so long, lived

off the "nectar" I boil up for them each week,
that they show me no semblance of fear or distrust—
they hover and feed near me with violent precision.

Portrait in Nightshade and Delayed Translation

In Saint Petersburg, on an autumn morning,
having been allowed an early entry
to the Hermitage, my family and I wandered
the empty hallways and corridors, virtually every space

adorned with famous paintings and artwork.
There must be a term for overloading on art.
One of Caravaggio's boys smirked at us,
his lips a red that betrayed a sloppy kiss

recently delivered, while across the room
the Virgin looked on with nothing but sorrow.
Even in museums, the drama is staged.
Bored, I left my family and, steered myself,

foolish moth, toward the light coming
from a rotunda. Before me, the empty stairs.
Ready to descend, ready to step outside
into the damp and chilly air, I felt

the centuries-old reflex kick in, that sense
of being watched. When I turned, I found
no one; instead, I was staring at *The Return
of the Prodigal Son.* I had studied it, written about it

as a student. But no amount of study could have
prepared me for the size of it, the darkness of it.
There, the son knelt before his father, his dirty foot
left for inspection. Something broke. As clichéd

as it sounds, something inside me broke, and
as if captured on film, I found myself slowly sinking
to my knees. The tears began without warning until soon
I was sobbing. What reflex betrays one like this?

What nerve agent did Rembrandt hide
within the dark shades of paint that he used?
What inside me had malfunctioned, had left me
kneeling and sobbing in a museum?

Prosto plakat. Prosto plakat. Osvobodi sebya,
said the guard as his hands steadied my shoulders.
He stood there repeating the phrase until
I stopped crying, until I was able to rise.

I'm not crazy, nor am I a very emotional man.
For most of my life, I have been called, correctly, cold.
As a student, I catalogued the techniques, carefully
analyzed this painting for a class on the "Dutch Masters."

Years later, having mustered the courage to tell
this ridiculous story, a friend who spoke Russian
translated the guard's words for me: *Just cry. Just cry.
Free yourself.* But free myself from what, exactly?

You see, I want this whole thing to be something
meaningful, my falling to my knees in front of a painting
by Rembrandt, a painting inspired by a parable
of forgiveness offered by a father to his lost son.

But nothing meaningful has presented itself. Even now,
after so much time has passed, I have no clue
what any of this means. I still haven't figured out
whether or not I am the lost son or the found.

Between the Dragon and the Phoenix

Fire in the heart, fire in the sky, the sun just
a smallish smudge resting on the horizon
out beyond the reef that breaks the waves,

fiery sun that waits for no one. I was little more
than a child when my father explained
that the mongrel is stronger than the thoroughbred,

that I was splendidly blended, genetically engineered
for survival. I somehow forgot this, misplaced this,
time eroding my memory as it erodes everything.

But go ask someone else to write a poem about Time.
Out over the bay, the sun is rising, and I am running
out of time. Each and every year, on my birthday,

I wake to watch the sunrise. I am superstitious.
And today, as in years past, it is not my father
but my father's father who comes to shout at me:

Whether you like it or not, you are a child of fire. You
descend from the Dragon, descend from the Phoenix.
Your blood is older than England, older than Castille.

Year after year, he says the same thing, this old man
dead long before I was born. So, I wake each year
on the day of my birth to watch the fire enter the sky

while being chastised by my dead grandfather.
Despite being a creature of fire, I stay near the water.
Why even try to avoid what can extinguish me?

There are times I can feel the fire flickering inside my frame.
The gulls are quarreling, the palm trees shimmering—
the world keeps spinning on its axis. Some say I have

nine lives. Others think me a machine. Neither is true.
The truth is rarely so conventional. Fire in my heart, fire
in my veins, I write this down for you and watch

as it goes up in flames. There are no paragraphs
wide enough to contain this fire, no stanzas
durable enough to house it. Blood of the Dragon,

blood of the Phoenix, I turn my head slowly
toward the East. I bow and call for another year.
I stand there and demand one more year.

Acknowledgments

Grateful acknowledgment is made to the editors of the following publications, where these poems—sometime in slightly different form—first appeared:

Academy of American Poets' *Poem-a-Day, Alaska Quarterly Review, The American Poetry Review, Anti-, Bennington Review, Blackbird, Boston College Magazine, Chelsea, The Collagist, Defunct, Four Way Review, The Georgia Review, The Greensboro Review, Harvard Review, The Hopkins Review, The Kenyon Review, Linebreak, The Massachusetts Review, Meridian, The Nation, The National Poetry Review, New England Review, North American Review, The Paris-American, The Paris Review, Ploughshares, Plume, Poet Lore, POETRY Magazine, Poetry International, Post Road, The Rupture, Salmagundi, Scoundrel Time, The Southern Review, Southwest Review, storySouth, Subtropics, TriQuarterly, Virginia Quarterly Review, The Yale Review, Waccamaw,* and *Waxwing.*

"Night Air" appeared as the poem of the day for November 5, 1999 at the Poetry Daily website (www.poems.com).

"August" has been reprinted in the Literature, Arts and Medicine database maintained by New York University, spring 2001 to the present.

"The Tree Frog" appeared as the poem of the day for April 12, 2004 at the Verse Daily website (www.versedaily.org).

"Invective" appeared in *Asian American Poetry: The Next Generation*, ed. Victoria Chang (University of Illinois Press, 2004).

"Proximity" and "Torn" appeared in *Legitimate Dangers: American Poets of the New Century*, eds. Michael Dumanis and Cate Marvin (Sarabande Books, 2006).

"Torn" appeared as the poem of the day for April 21, 2004 at the Poetry Daily website (www.poems.com).

"Torn" appeared as a limited-edition, fine letterpress broadside (Mad River Press, 2004).

"Torn" has been reprinted in the Literature, Arts and Medicine database maintained by New York University, spring 2005 to the present.

"Sepsis" appeared in *Best American Poetry 2008*, ed. Charles Wright, series ed. David Lehman (Scribner, 2008).

"In the Cutting Room," "Inheritance," "Or Something Like That," "The Bridge," and "Torn" were reprinted in *The Swallow Anthology of New American Poets*, ed. David Yezzi (Swallow Press/Ohio University Press, 2009).

"Or Something Like That" and "Paying Attention" appeared in *Before the Door of God: An Anthology of Devotional Poetry*, eds. Jay Hopler and Kimberly Johnson (Yale University Press, 2010).

"*Precatio simplex*" appeared in *The Best American Poetry 2017*, ed. Natasha Trethewey, series ed. David Lehman (Scribner, 2017).

"The Point" was broadcast on *The Slowdown*, hosted by Ada Limón (May 24, 2022).

For their invaluable help and friendship, I would like to thank James Allen Hall and Tomás Q. Morín. I would also like to thank my family and friends for the support, both large and small, they have given me. I especially want to thank my editor, Martha Rhodes, and all of the people that constitute Four Way Books for their continued support of my work.

About the Author

C. Dale Young practices medicine full-time and teaches in the Warren Wilson MFA Program for Writers. He is the author of *The Affliction* (Four Way Books, 2018), a novel in stories, and the poetry collections *The Day Underneath the Day* (Northwestern, 2001); *The Second Person* (Four Way Books, 2007), a finalist for the Lambda Literary Award in Poetry; *Torn* (Four Way Books, 2011), named one of the best poetry collections of 2011 by National Public Radio; *The Halo* (Four Way Books, 2016), a finalist for the Lambda Literary Award in Poetry; and *Prometeo* (Four Way Books, 2021). He is a previous recipient of the Grolier Prize, the Stanley W. Lindberg Award for Literary Editing, and the 2017/2018 Hanes Award in Poetry given by the Fellowship of Southern Writers to honor a poet at mid-career. A fellow of the National Endowment for the Arts, the John Simon Guggenheim Memorial Foundation, and the Rockefeller Foundation, his poems and short fiction have appeared widely. He lives in San Francisco.

We are also grateful to those individuals who participated in our Build a Book Program. They are:

Anonymous (14), Robert Abrams, Debra Allbery, Nancy Allen, Michael Ansara, Kathy Aponick, Jean Ball, Sally Ball, Jill Bialosky, Sophie Cabot Black, Laurel Blossom, Tommye Blount, Karen and David Blumenthal, Jonathan Blunk, Lee Briccetti, Jane Martha Brox, Mary Lou Buschi, Anthony Cappo, Carla and Steven Carlson, Robin Rosen Chang, Liza Charlesworth, Peter Coyote, Elinor Cramer, Kwame Dawes, Michael Anna de Armas, Brian Komei Dempster, Renko and Stuart Dempster, Matthew DeNichilo, Rosalynde Vas Dias, Patrick Donnelly, Charles R. Douthat, Lynn Emanuel, Blas Falconer, Laura Fjeld, Carolyn Forché, Helen Fremont and Donna Thagard, Debra Gitterman, Dorothy Tapper Goldman, Alison Granucci, Elizabeth T. Gray Jr., Naomi Guttman and Jonathan Mead, Jeffrey Harrison, KT Herr, Carlie Hoffman, Melissa Hotchkiss, Thomas and Autumn Howard, Catherine Hoyser, Elizabeth Jackson, Linda Susan Jackson, Jessica Jacobs, Deborah Jonas-Walsh, Jennifer Just, Voki Kalfayan, Maeve Kinkead, Victoria Korth, David Lee and Jamila Trindle, Rodney Terich Leonard, Howard Levy, Owen Lewis and Susan Ennis, Eve Linn, Matthew Lippman, Ralph and Mary Ann Lowen, Maja Lukic, Neal Lulofs, Anthony Lyons, Ricardo Alberto Maldonado, Trish Marshall, Donna Masini, Deborah McAlister, Carol Moldaw, Michael and Nancy Murphy, Kimberly Nunes, Matthew Olzmann and Vievee Francis, Veronica Patterson, Patrick Phillips, Robert Pinsky, Megan Pinto, Kevin Prufer, Anna Duke Reach, Paula Rhodes, Yoana Setzer, James Shalek, Soraya Shalforoosh, Peggy Shinner, Joan Silber, Jane Simon, Debra Spark, Donna Spruijt-Metz, Arlene Stang, Page Hill Starzinger, Catherine Stearns, Yerra Sugarman, Arthur Sze, Laurence Tancredi, Marjorie and Lew Tesser, Peter Turchi, Connie Voisine, Susan Walton, Martha Webster and Robert Fuentes, Calvin Wei, Allison Benis White, Lauren Yaffe, and Rolf Yngve.